P9-CKF-306

Interactions 1

SENTENCE DEVELOPMENT AND
INTRODUCTION TO THE PARAGRAPH **WRITING**

Cheryl Pavlik
Margaret Keenan Segal

Lawrence J. Zwier
Contributor, Focus on Testing

Meredith Pike-Baky
Writing Strand Leader

McGraw
Hill

Interactions 1 Writing, Silver Edition

Published by McGraw-Hill ESL/ELT, a business unit of The McGraw-Hill Companies, Inc., 1221 Avenue of the Americas, New York, NY 10020. Copyright © 2007 by The McGraw-Hill Companies, Inc. All rights reserved. No part of this publication may be reproduced or distributed in any form or by any means, or stored in a database or retrieval system, without the prior written consent of The McGraw-Hill Companies, Inc., including, but not limited to, in any network or other electronic storage or transmission, or broadcast for distance learning.

ISBN 13: 978-0-07-353385-8 (Student Book)
ISBN 10: 0-07-353385-8
1 2 3 4 5 6 7 8 9 10 VNH 11 10 09 08 07 06

Editorial director: Erik Gundersen
Series editor: Valerie Kelemen
Developmental editor: Jennifer Wilson Cooper
Production manager: Juanita Thompson
Production coordinator: Vanessa Nuttry, James D. Gwyn
Cover designer: Robin Locke Monda
Interior designer: Nesbitt Graphics, Inc.
Artists: Emma Lazarus
Photo researcher: Photoquick Research

The credits section for this book begins on page 192 and is considered an extension of the copyright page.

Cover photo: Steve Allen/Creatas Images

A Special Thank You

The Interactions/Mosaic Silver Edition team wishes to thank our extended team: teachers, students, administrators, and teacher trainers, all of whom contributed invaluably to the making of this edition.

Macarena Aguilar, **North Harris College**, Houston, Texas ■ Mohamad Al-Alam, **Imam Mohammad University**, Riyadh, Saudi Arabia ■ Faisal M. Al Mohanna Abaalkhail, **King Saud University**, Riyadh, Saudi Arabia; Amal Al-Toaimy, **Women's College, Prince Sultan University**, Riyadh, Saudi Arabia ■ Douglas Arroliga, **Ave Maria University**, Managua, Nicaragua ■ Fairlie Atkinson, **Sungkyunkwan University**, Seoul, Korea ■ Jose R. Bahamonde, **Miami-Dade Community College**, Miami, Florida ■ John Ball, **Universidad de las Americas**, Mexico City, Mexico ■ Steven Bell, **Universidad la Salle**, Mexico City, Mexico ■ Damian Benstead, **Sungkyunkwan University**, Seoul, Korea ■ Paul Cameron, **National Chengchi University**, Taipei, Taiwan R.O.C. ■ Sun Chang, **Soongsil University**, Seoul, Korea ■ Grace Chao, **Soochow University**, Taipei, Taiwan R.O.C. ■ Chien Ping Chen, **Hua Fan University**, Taipei, Taiwan R.O.C. ■ Selma Chen, **Chihlee Institute of Technology**, Taipei, Taiwan R.O.C. ■ Sylvia Chiu, **Soochow University**, Taipei, Taiwan R.O.C. ■ Mary Colonna, **Columbia University**, New York, New York ■ Lee Culver, **Miami-Dade Community College,** Miami, Florida ■ Joy Durighello, **City College of San Francisco**, San Francisco, California ■ Isabel Del Valle, **ULATINA**, San Jose, Costa Rica ■ Linda Emerson, **Sogang University**, Seoul, Korea ■ Esther Entin, **Miami-Dade Community College**, Miami, Florida ■ Glenn Farrier, **Gakushuin Women's College**, Tokyo, Japan ■ Su Wei Feng, Taipei, Taiwan R.O.C. ■ Judith Garcia, **Miami-Dade Community College**, Miami, Florida ■ Maxine Gillway, **United Arab Emirates University**, Al Ain, United Arab Emirates ■ Colin Gullberg, **Soochow University**, Taipei, Taiwan R.O.C. ■ Natasha Haugnes, **Academy of Art University**, San Francisco, California ■ Barbara Hockman, **City College of San Francisco**, San Francisco, California ■ Jinyoung Hong, **Sogang University**, Seoul, Korea ■ Sherry Hsieh, **Christ's College**, Taipei, Taiwan R.O.C. ■ Yu-shen Hsu, **Soochow University**, Taipei, Taiwan R.O.C. ■ Cheung Kai-Chong, **Shih-Shin University**, Taipei, Taiwan R.O.C. ■ Leslie Kanberg, **City College of San Francisco**, San Francisco, California ■ Gregory Keech, **City College of San Francisco**, San Francisco, California ■ Susan Kelly, **Sogang University**, Seoul, Korea ■ Myoungsuk Kim, **Soongsil University**, Seoul, Korea ■ Youngsuk Kim, **Soongsil University**, Seoul, Korea ■ Roy Langdon, **Sungkyunkwan University**, Seoul, Korea ■ Rocio Lara, **University of Costa Rica**, San Jose, Costa Rica ■ Insung Lee, **Soongsil University**, Seoul, Korea ■ Andy Leung, **National Tsing Hua University**, Taipei, Taiwan R.O.C. ■ Elisa Li Chan, **University of Costa Rica**, San Jose, Costa Rica ■ Elizabeth Lorenzo, **Universidad Internacional de las Americas**, San Jose, Costa Rica

■ Cheryl Magnant, **Sungkyunkwan University**, Seoul, Korea ■ Narciso Maldonado Iuit, **Escuela Tecnica Electricista**, Mexico City, Mexico ■ Shaun Manning, **Hankuk University of Foreign Studies**, Seoul, Korea ■ Yoshiko Matsubayashi, **Tokyo International University**, Saitama, Japan ■ Scott Miles, **Sogang University**, Seoul, Korea ■ William Mooney, **Chinese Culture University**, Taipei, Taiwan R.O.C. ■ Jeff Moore, **Sungkyunkwan University**, Seoul, Korea ■ Mavelin de Moreno, **Lehnsen Roosevelt School**, Guatemala City, Guatemala ■ Ahmed Motala, **University of Sharjah**, Sharjah, United Arab Emirates ■ Carlos Navarro, **University of Costa Rica**, San Jose, Costa Rica ■ Dan Neal, **Chih Chien University**, Taipei, Taiwan R.O.C. ■ Margarita Novo, **University of Costa Rica**, San Jose, Costa Rica ■ Karen O'Neill, **San Jose State University**, San Jose, California ■ Linda O'Roke, **City College of San Francisco**, San Francisco, California ■ Martha Padilla, **Colegio de Bachilleres de Sinaloa,** Culiacan, Mexico ■ Allen Quesada, **University of Costa Rica**, San Jose, Costa Rica ■ Jim Rogge, **Broward Community College**, Ft. Lauderdale, Florida ■ Marge Ryder, **City College of San Francisco**, San Francisco, California ■ Gerardo Salas, **University of Costa Rica**, San Jose, Costa Rica ■ Shigeo Sato, **Tamagawa University**, Tokyo, Japan ■ Lynn Schneider, **City College of San Francisco**, San Francisco, California ■ Devan Scoble, **Sungkyunkwan University**, Seoul, Korea ■ Maryjane Scott, **Soongsil University**, Seoul, Korea ■ Ghaida Shaban, **Makassed Philanthropic School**, Beirut, Lebanon ■ Maha Shalok, **Makassed Philanthropic School**, Beirut, Lebanon ■ John Shannon, **University of Sharjah**, Sharjah, United Arab Emirates ■ Elsa Sheng, **National Technology College of Taipei**, Taipei, Taiwan R.O.C. ■ Ye-Wei Sheng, **National Taipei College of Business**, Taipei, Taiwan R.O.C. ■ Emilia Sobaja, **University of Costa Rica**, San Jose, Costa Rica ■ You-Souk Yoon, **Sungkyunkwan University**, Seoul, Korea ■ Shanda Stromfield, **San Jose State University**, San Jose, California ■ Richard Swingle, **Kansai Gaidai College**, Osaka, Japan ■ Carol Sung, **Christ's College**, Taipei, Taiwan R.O.C. ■ Jeng-Yih Tim Hsu, **National Kaohsiung First University of Science and Technology**, Kaohsiung, Taiwan R.O.C. ■ Shinichiro Torikai, **Rikkyo University**, Tokyo, Japan ■ Sungsoon Wang, **Sogang University**, Seoul, Korea ■ Kathleen Wolf, **City College of San Francisco**, San Francisco, California ■ Sean Wray, **Waseda University International**, Tokyo, Japan ■ Belinda Yanda, **Academy of Art University**, San Francisco, California ■ Su Huei Yang, **National Taipei College of Business**, Taipei, Taiwan R.O.C. ■ Tzu Yun Yu, **Chungyu Institute of Technology**, Taipei, Taiwan R.O.C.

Interactions/Mosaic **Silver Edition** is a fully-integrated, 18-book academic skills series. Language proficiencies are articulated from the beginning through advanced levels <u>within</u> each of the four language skill strands. Chapter themes articulate <u>across</u> the four skill strands to systematically recycle content, vocabulary, and grammar.

NEW to the Silver Edition:

- **World's most popular and comprehensive academic skills series—** thoroughly updated for today's global learners
- **Writing Articulation Chart** outlines how the Interactions/Mosaic writing program leads students from sentence building to academic essay writing
- **Writing revision process** focuses on *Revising* (focusing on the big picture) and *Editing* (focusing on the word and sentence level)
- **New strategies and activities for the TOEFL® iBT** build invaluable test taking skills
- **New "Best Practices" approach** promotes excellence in language teaching

NEW to Interactions 1 Writing:

- **All new content:**—Chapter 10 Sports
- **Transparent chapter structure** with consistent part headings, activity labeling, and clear guidance—strengthens the academic experience:

  Part 1: Before You Write
  Part 2: Developing Writing Skills
  Part 3: Revising and Editing
  Part 4: Expansion Activities

- **Systematically structured, multi-step *Writing Process*** culminates in a *Writing Product* task
- **New and direct connections between writing and grammar** tie the writing skill in focus with the grammar structures needed to develop each writing skill
- **New communicative activities** invite students to interact meaningfully with target words to build vocabulary skills for writing
- **New self-evaluation rubric** for each chapter supports the learner as he or she builds confidence and autonomy in academic writing

---

* TOEFL is a registered trademark of Education Testing Service (ETS). This publication is not endorsed or approved by ETS.

Our Interactions/Mosaic Silver Edition team has produced an edition that focuses on Best Practices, principles that contribute to excellent language teaching and learning. Our team of writers, editors, and teacher consultants has identified the following six interconnected Best Practices:

Making Use of Academic Content

Materials and tasks based on academic content and experiences give learning real purpose. Students explore real world issues, discuss academic topics, and study content-based and thematic materials.

Organizing Information

Students learn to organize thoughts and notes through a variety of graphic organizers that accommodate diverse learning and thinking styles.

Scaffolding Instruction

A scaffold is a physical structure that facilitates construction of a building. Similarly, scaffolding instruction is a tool used to facilitate language learning in the form of predictable and flexible tasks. Some examples include oral or written modeling by the teacher or students, placing information in a larger framework, and reinterpretation.

Activating Prior Knowledge

Students can better understand new spoken or written material when they connect to the content. Activating prior knowledge allows students to tap into what they already know, building on this knowledge, and stirring a curiosity for more knowledge.

Interacting with Others

Activities that promote human interaction in pair work, small group work, and whole class activities present opportunities for real world contact and real world use of language.

Cultivating Critical Thinking

Strategies for critical thinking are taught explicitly. Students learn tools that promote critical thinking skills crucial to success in the academic world.

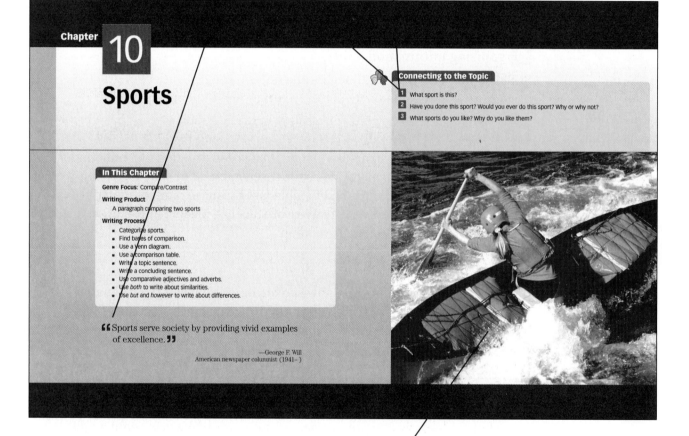

Chapter

10

Sports

Connecting to the Topic

1. What sport is this?
2. Have you done this sport? Would you ever do this sport? Why or why not?
3. What sports do you like? Why do you like them?

In This Chapter

Genre Focus: Compare/Contrast

Writing Product
  A paragraph comparing two sports

Writing Process
- Categorize sports.
- Find bases of comparison.
- Use a Venn diagram.
- Use a comparison table.
- Write a topic sentence.
- Write a concluding sentence.
- Use comparative adjectives and adverbs.
- Use *both* to write about similarities.
- Use *but* and *however* to write about differences.

❝Sports serve society by providing vivid examples of excellence. ❞

—George F. Will
American newspaper columnist (1941–)

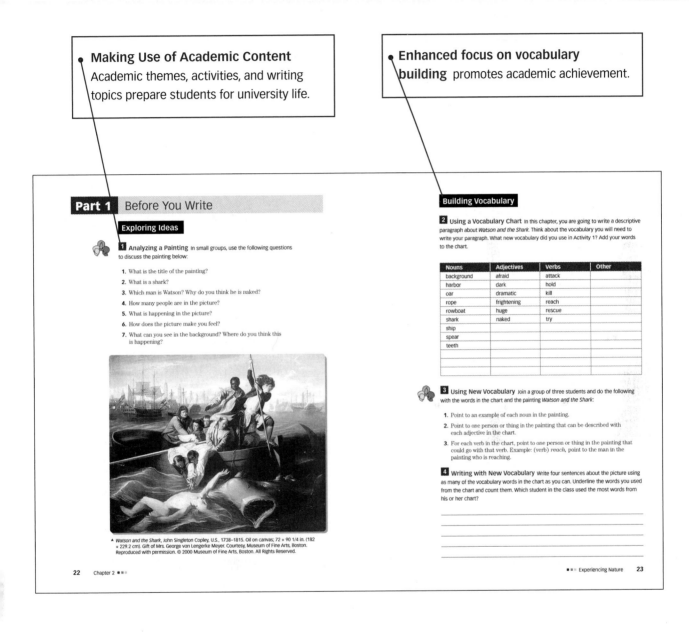

Making Use of Academic Content
Academic themes, activities, and writing topics prepare students for university life.

Enhanced focus on vocabulary building promotes academic achievement.

Part 1   Before You Write

Exploring Ideas

1 Analyzing a Painting In small groups, use the following questions to discuss the painting below:

1. What is the title of the painting?
2. What is a shark?
3. Which man is Watson? Why do you think he is naked?
4. How many people are in the picture?
5. What is happening in the picture?
6. How does the picture make you feel?
7. What can you see in the background? Where do you think this is happening?

▲ *Watson and the Shark*, John Singleton Copley, U.S., 1738–1815. Oil on canvas; 72 × 90 1/4 in. (182 × 229.2 cm). Gift of Mrs. George von Lengerke Meyer. Courtesy, Museum of Fine Arts, Boston. Reproduced with permission. © 2000 Museum of Fine Arts, Boston. All Rights Reserved.

Building Vocabulary

2 Using a Vocabulary Chart In this chapter, you are going to write a descriptive paragraph about *Watson and the Shark*. Think about the vocabulary you will need to write your paragraph. What new vocabulary did you use in Activity 1? Add your words to the chart.

Nouns	Adjectives	Verbs	Other
background	afraid	attack	
harbor	dark	hold	
oar	dramatic	kill	
rope	frightening	reach	
rowboat	huge	rescue	
shark	naked	try	
ship			
spear			
teeth			

3 Using New Vocabulary Join a group of three students and do the following with the words in the chart and the painting *Watson and the Shark*:

1. Point to an example of each noun in the painting.
2. Point to one person or thing in the painting that can be described with each adjective in the chart.
3. For each verb in the chart, point to one person or thing in the painting that could go with that verb. Example: (verb) *reach*, point to the man in the painting who is reaching.

4 Writing with New Vocabulary Write four sentences about the picture using as many of the vocabulary words in the chart as you can. Underline the words you used from the chart and count them. Which student in the class used the most words from his or her chart?

_____
_____
_____
_____
_____
_____

Organizing Information
Graphic organizers provide tools for organizing information and ideas.

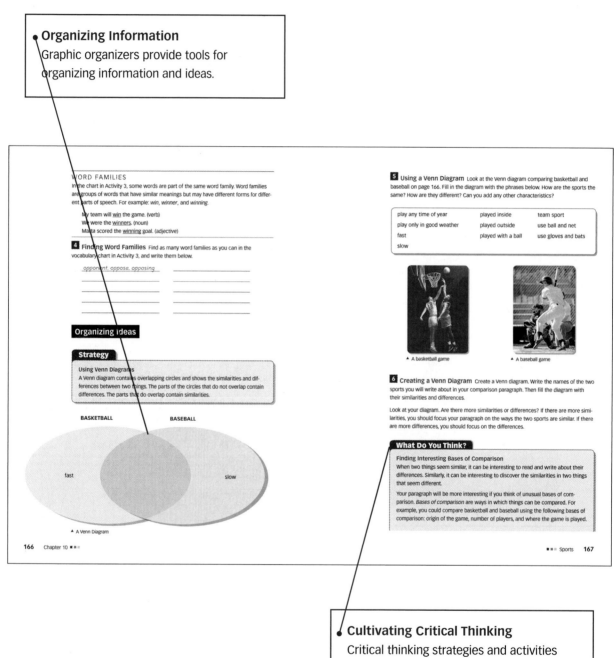

WORD FAMILIES

In the chart in Activity 3, some words are part of the same word family. Word families are groups of words that have similar meanings but may have different forms for different parts of speech. For example: *win, winner,* and *winning*.

My team will <u>win</u> the game. (verb)
We were the <u>winners</u>. (noun)
Marta scored the <u>winning</u> goal. (adjective)

4 **Finding Word Families** Find as many word families as you can in the vocabulary chart in Activity 3, and write them below.

opponent, oppose, opposing

_____ _____
_____ _____
_____ _____
_____ _____

Organizing Ideas

Strategy

Using Venn Diagrams
A Venn diagram contains overlapping circles and shows the similarities and differences between two things. The parts of the circles that do not overlap contain differences. The parts that do overlap contain similarities.

BASKETBALL   BASEBALL

fast   slow

▲ A Venn Diagram

5 **Using a Venn Diagram** Look at the Venn diagram comparing basketball and baseball on page 166. Fill in the diagram with the phrases below. How are the sports the same? How are they different? Can you add any other characteristics?

play any time of year	played inside	team sport
play only in good weather	played outside	use ball and net
fast	played with a ball	use gloves and bats
slow		

▲ A basketball game   ▲ A baseball game

6 **Creating a Venn Diagram** Create a Venn diagram. Write the names of the two sports you will write about in your comparison paragraph. Then fill the diagram with their similarities and differences.

Look at your diagram. Are there more similarities or differences? If there are more similarities, you should focus your paragraph on the ways the two sports are similar. If there are more differences, you should focus on the differences.

What Do You Think?

Finding Interesting Bases of Comparison
When two things seem similar, it can be interesting to read and write about their differences. Similarly, it can be interesting to discover the similarities in two things that seem different.

Your paragraph will be more interesting if you think of unusual bases of comparison. *Bases of comparison* are ways in which things can be compared. For example, you could compare basketball and baseball using the following bases of comparison: origin of the game, number of players, and where the game is played.

Cultivating Critical Thinking
Critical thinking strategies and activities equip students with the skills they need for academic achievement.

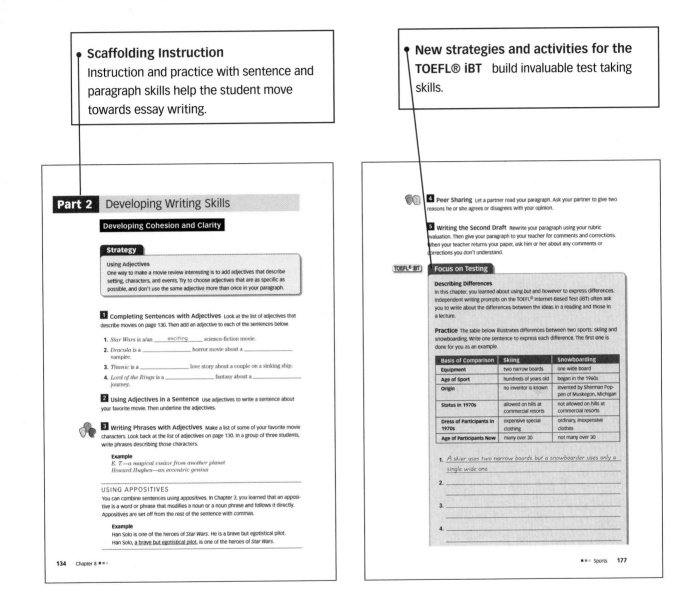

Scaffolding Instruction

Instruction and practice with sentence and paragraph skills help the student move towards essay writing.

New strategies and activities for the TOEFL® iBT build invaluable test taking skills.

Part 2 Developing Writing Skills

Developing Cohesion and Clarity

Strategy

Using Adjectives
One way to make a movie review interesting is to add adjectives that describe setting, characters, and events. Try to choose adjectives that are as specific as possible, and don't use the same adjective more than once in your paragraph.

1 Completing Sentences with Adjectives Look at the list of adjectives that describe movies on page 130. Then add an adjective to each of the sentences below.

1. *Star Wars* is a/an _____exciting_____ science-fiction movie.
2. *Dracula* is a _____ horror movie about a _____ vampire.
3. *Titanic* is a _____ love story about a couple on a sinking ship.
4. *Lord of the Rings* is a _____ fantasy about a _____ journey.

2 Using Adjectives in a Sentence Use adjectives to write a sentence about your favorite movie. Then underline the adjectives.

3 Writing Phrases with Adjectives Make a list of some of your favorite movie characters. Look back at the list of adjectives on page 130. In a group of three students, write phrases describing those characters.

Example
E. T.—a magical visitor from another planet
Howard Hughes—an eccentric genius

USING APPOSITIVES
You can combine sentences using appositives. In Chapter 3, you learned that an appositive is a word or phrase that modifies a noun or a noun phrase and follows it directly. Appositives are set off from the rest of the sentence with commas.

Example
Han Solo is one of the heroes of *Star Wars*. He is a brave but egotistical pilot.
Han Solo, a brave but egotistical pilot, is one of the heroes of *Star Wars*.

---

4 Peer Sharing Let a partner read your paragraph. Ask your partner to give two reasons he or she agrees or disagrees with your opinion.

5 Writing the Second Draft Rewrite your paragraph using your rubric evaluation. Then give your paragraph to your teacher for comments and corrections. When your teacher returns your paper, ask him or her about any comments or corrections you don't understand.

TOEFL® iBT | **Focus on Testing**

Describing Differences
In this chapter, you learned about using *but* and *however* to express differences. Independent writing prompts on the TOEFL® Internet-Based Test (iBT) often ask you to write about the differences between the ideas in a reading and those in a lecture.

Practice The table below illustrates differences between two sports: skiing and snowboarding. Write one sentence to express each difference. The first one is done for you as an example.

Basis of Comparison	Skiing	Snowboarding
Equipment	two narrow boards	one wide board
Age of Sport	hundreds of years old	began in the 1960s
Origin	no inventor is known	invented by Sherman Poppen of Muskegon, Michigan
Status in 1970s	allowed on hills at commercial resorts	not allowed on hills at commercial resorts
Dress of Participants in 1970s	expensive special clothing	ordinary, inexpensive clothes
Age of Participants Now	many over 30	not many over 30

1. *A skier uses two narrow boards, but a snowboarder uses only a single wide one.*
2. _____
3. _____
4. _____

Chapter	Writing Product	Vocabulary Development	Idea Development/ Organizing Skills
1 **Academic Life Around the World**	A **descriptive** paragraph about a classmate	Using a vocabulary chart Developing vocabulary in a semantic field: daily activities	Interviewing a classmate Ordering information in a paragraph Using a graphic organizer Writing topic sentences
2 **Experiencing Nature**	A **descriptive** paragraph about a painting	Using an illustration to generate vocabulary Generating vocabulary through discussion	Discussing a painting Ordering information from general to specific Grouping details in spatial order
3 **Living to Eat or Eating to Live?**	A **descriptive** paragraph about holiday foods	Generating vocabulary through discussion Developing vocabulary in a semantic field: words to describe foods	Free writing Ordering information from general to specific Using a graphic organizer to determine levels of detail Writing topic sentences

Grammar	Editing Skills	Critical Thinking	Focus on Testing
Using connectors: *and*, *but*, and *so* Using *also* to add information	Revising for content: topic sentence, focus, and grouping of related ideas Editing for form: paragraph format, third person singular, negative verb forms, and capitalization	Distinguishing fact and opinion Choosing relevant interview questions	
Using descriptive adjectives Using prepositional phrases Unifying a paragraph with pronouns Using the present continuous Using *a*, *an*, and *the*	Revising for content: inclusion of important details, order of information, use of adjectives Editing for form: Use of articles, paragraph and sentence form	Analyzing artwork Distinguishing general and specific Determining spacial order	
Using count and noncount nouns Giving examples with *such as* Using appositives Punctuating lists Spelling third-person singular verbs	Revising for content: adding appositives and *such as* Editing for form: use of commas in lists, plural nouns, and third person singular	Classifying foods Analyzing a graphic organizer Distinguishing general and specific information Evaluating nouns: count or noncount Identifying your strengths and challenges	

Chapter	Writing Product	Vocabulary Development	Idea Development/ Organizing Skills
4 In the community	An **informative** letter to a friend	Generating new vocabulary through free writing Developing vocabulary in a semantic field: activities in a place; direction words	Organizing paragraphs in a letter Using a graphic organizer to write directions
5 Home	A personal **narrative**	Generating new vocabulary through discussion Developing vocabulary in a semantic field: life events	Using a time line to organize information Choosing a topic Limiting information Writing topic sentences
6 Cultures of the World	The conclusion of a folktale **narrative**	Generating vocabulary from reading Generating vocabulary through discussion	Reading and discussing a folk tale Using a plot diagram Understanding the elements of a story

Grammar	Editing Skills	Critical Thinking	Focus on Testing
Using the present tense and *be going to* for future Using prepositions of location, direction, and distance Using *there*, *it*, and *they*	Revising for content: paragraph division Editing for form: letter format	Selecting the correct verb tense Evaluating community services Relating directions to a map	
Using the past tense Combining sentences with *because* Using *before*, *after*, *when*, and *as soon as*	Revising for content: combining ideas with *but*, so, and *and* Editing for Form: punctuating dependent clauses	Brainstorming ideas Evaluating a theory by applying it to life experience	
Using *when* and *while* Varying time words: *when*, *while*, *before*, *after*, *then*, and *as soon as*	Revising for content: clarity, relevance, and sequence Editing for form: using editing symbols	Ordering events Proposing an original ending to a folktale Interpreting the moral of a folktale Evaluating elements of a story	TOEFL® IBT Borrowing vocabulary from a reading

Chapter	Writing Product	Vocabulary Development	Idea Development/ Organizing Skills
7 Health	An **informational** paragraph about health treatments	Developing vocabulary in a semantic field: health Using suffixes to generate new vocabulary	Using an idea map Writing topic sentences
8 Entertainment and the Media	A one-paragraph movie review and **analysis**	Developing vocabulary in a semantic field: movies and characters Identifying positive and negative adjectives	Using a story web Identifying the elements of a story
9 Social Life	A **narrative** paragraph about a classmate	Developing vocabulary in a semantic field: leisure–time activities Building vocabulary with suffixes	Interviewing a classmate Choosing a method of organizing information Writing topic and concluding sentences
10 Sports	A paragraph **comparing** two sports	Developing vocabulary in a semantic field: sports Generating new vocabulary with word families	Using a Venn diagram Using a comparison table Writing topic and concluding sentences

Grammar	Editing Skills	Critical Thinking	Focus on Testing
Using restrictive relative clauses Using *in addition*, *however*, *for example* Giving reasons with *because* and infinitives of purpose	Revising for content: relevance and transitions Editing for form: editing symbols and punctuation with *and* and *but*	Defining broad terms Brainstorming and evaluating ideas Contrasting modern and traditional medicine	**TOEFL® IBT** Using transition words
Using the historical present tense Using appositives Using adjectives to describe character and setting	Revising for content: appositives and relevance Editing for form: spelling of present and past participles, capitalization	Classifying adjectives as positive or negative Categorizing movies by genre Analyzing movie choices	**TOEFL® IBT** Using the historical present tense
Choosing the correct verb tense Using transitional words and phrases: *also*, *in addition*, *in fact*, and *however* Expressing cause and effect with *so...that*	Revising for content: combining ideas Editing for form: connecting words, and comparatives	Ordering ideas Identifying poor concluding sentences Analyzing how you spend your time	**TOEFL® IBT** Managing time
Using comparative adjectives and adverbs Using *both* to write about similarities Using *but* and *however* to write about differences	Revising for content: topic sentence and combining sentences Editing for form: connecting words and comparative structures	Categorizing sports Finding bases of comparison	**TOEFL® IBT** Describing differences

Academic Life Around the World

❝ The foundation of every state is the education of its youth. ❞

—Diogenes Laertius
Greek biographer (c. 250)

Connecting to the Topic

1 Is this classroom environment similar to yours? Why or why not?

2 What are some other types of classroom settings?

3 What type of classroom environment do you prefer? Why?

Exploring Ideas

1 Reviewing Interview Questions A reporter for a school newspaper is writing an article about new students on campus. Read the questions he will ask the students.

1. What is your name?
2. Where are you from?
3. What classes are you taking?
4. What do you like about this school?
5. What do you like to do in your free time?
6. What are your plans for the future?

▲ Interviewing a classmate

2 Writing Interview Questions In this chapter, you are going to interview a classmate and write a descriptive paragraph about him or her. Write some questions for your interview. Use some of the questions above, and write three new questions.

 3 Sharing Your Interview Questions Your teacher will write some of your questions on the board. Discuss them as a class. Are they good questions to ask? Now look at your own questions. Are they good questions? Make any changes you think are necessary.

4 Interviewing Someone Look at the questions on the board and the questions you wrote. Choose the ten questions you like the best. Then choose a partner, and interview him or her using the ten questions you chose. Write your partner's answers after each question.

Building Vocabulary

Strategy

Using Vocabulary Charts
One way to learn new words is to make vocabulary charts. For example, you can make a chart that lists new words by categories or topics.

 5 Using a Vocabulary Chart Work in groups of four or five. Share the words you used for your interview with the other members of your group. Decide which words are the most important for you, and add them to the chart below. Some words are given as examples.

Classes	Free-time Activities	Future Plans	Other New Vocabulary
art	drawing	artist	helpful

Organizing Ideas

Strategy

Facts and Opinions
It is important to understand the difference between fact and opinion. A fact is a statement that can be proven: something that everyone would agree on. An opinion is someone's idea. It may or may not be true. For example, these statements are facts: *Today's date is March 11. Paris is the capital of France.* These statements are opinions: *Today is a wonderful day. Paris is a beautiful city.*

6 **Distinguishing Fact and Opinion** A student interviewed Yara Haider for her paragraph. Look at the student's questions and notes. Write *F* (fact) next to questions about facts and *O* (opinion) next to questions about opinions.

1. _F_ What is your name?
   Yara Haider

2. _____ Where are you from?
   Aleppo, Syria.

3. _____ How old are you?
   Nineteen.

4. _____ Why are you studying in Beirut?
   Because my father is Lebanese, and I want to learn about Lebanon.

5. _____ What classes are you taking?
   English, art, history, and fashion design.

6. _____ Why are you studying English?
   Because fashion design is an international business, so I need to be able to communicate in English.

7. _____ What do you think about Lebanese Technical College?
   I think the classes are excellent, the students are friendly, and the teachers are helpful.

8. _____ What do you dislike about this college?
   I think the food in the cafeteria is terrible, and the campus needs some more trees.

9. _____ What do you do in your free time?
   I like to draw and to go folk dancing.

10. _____ What are your plans for the future?
    I plan to be a fashion designer.

Using Graphic Organizers

Strategy

Graphic Organizers
Sometimes it is helpful to use a diagram to organize information before writing. This kind of diagram is called a *graphic organizer*. There are many different types of graphic organizers, but they all have one thing in common—they help us to see how different pieces of information are connected or related to each other. They can also show us when information is missing or unnecessary.

7 **Analyzing a Graphic Organizer** The graphic organizer below contains notes from the interview in Activity 6. Review the graphic organizer and discuss the following questions in groups of three:

1. The information is organized in several groups. What do the groups represent?
2. How does the diagram show that information is related?
3. What information from the interview is not included in the diagram?
4. Where should it go? How do you know?

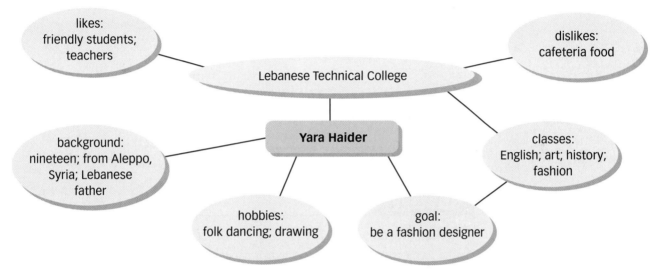

8 **Creating a Graphic Organizer** Write *F* (fact) or *O* (opinion) in front of the questions that you asked in Activity 4. Then use the information to create a graphic organizer like the one above.

 9 **Sharing Your Graphic Organizer** Show your graphic organizer to the person you interviewed. Does she or he want to add any information?

Writing Topic Sentences

Strategy

Functions and Characteristics of a Topic Sentence
When you write a topic sentence, keep the following in mind:

- It tells the reader the main idea of a paragraph.
- Every sentence in the paragraph relates to it.
- It should not be too general or too specific.
- It should not use phrases such as *I am going to write about . . .* or *This paragraph is about . . .*

10 **Choosing the Best Topic Sentence** Read the sentences below. Choose the one that would be a good topic sentence for the paragraph about Yara Haider.

    a. Yara Haider is a woman.
    b. Yara Haider doesn't like the food in the cafeteria.
    c. Yara Haider is one of many new students at Lebanese Technical College.

11 **Writing a Draft Topic Sentence** Write a draft topic sentence for the paragraph you will write about a classmate. Remember that this is just a draft. Once you write your paragraph, you might want to change your topic sentence.

Part 2 | Developing Writing Skills

Developing Cohesion and Clarity

Strategy

Connecting Ideas
Good writers connect the ideas in their paragraphs. A paragraph with connected ideas is cohesive. It is clear and easy to read.

1 **Analyzing Connectors** Look at the paragraph about Yara Haider on page 9, and circle the words *and, but, so,* and *also.* Then answer the following questions in groups.

    1. Which words add information?
        What information is added?

    2. Which word introduces a result?
        What result is introduced?

    3. Which word indicates contrasting information?
        What information is contrasted?

Yara Haider is one of many new students at Lebanese Technical College. She is nineteen (and) from Aleppo, Syria. Her father is Lebanese, so she is studying in Beirut in order to learn about his native country and culture. She is living in Beirut with her aunt. She is studying to be a fashion designer. Yara likes LTC very much. She likes the friendly students and the helpful teachers. She also thinks her classes are excellent, but she doesn't like the food in the cafeteria.

▲ Yara Haider

USING *AND* TO CONNECT PHRASES AND SENTENCES

When you want to say two things about a subject, use the word *and* to connect the information.

Sometimes *and* connects phrases that have the same verb. There is no need to repeat the subject or verb after *and*.

Examples

Yara <u>is</u> studying English. Yara <u>is</u> studying art.
Yara is studying <u>English and art.</u>

Yoshi <u>likes</u> reading. Yoshi <u>likes</u> watching television.
Yoshi likes <u>reading and watching television</u>.

Sometimes *and* connects phrases that have different verbs. There is no need to repeat the subject after *and*.

Examples

Yara Haider <u>is</u> 19. Yara Haider <u>plans</u> to be a fashion designer.
Yara Haider <u>is 19 and plans to be</u> a fashion designer.

Yoshi <u>works</u> in the morning. Yoshi <u>goes</u> to school at night.
Yoshi <u>works in the morning and goes to school</u> at night.

---

2 **Connecting Sentences with *And*** Look at the pairs of sentences below. For each pair, write a new sentence by connecting the two sentences with *and*.

1. Ming Su is 26 years old.
Ming Su comes from Taiwan.
Ming Su is 26 years old and comes from Taiwan.

2. Amelia eats breakfast in the cafeteria.
Amelia eats lunch in the cafeteria.

_____

3. Reiko is 19 years old.
Reiko likes music a lot.

_____

4. Salma is married.
Salma is a student.

_____

5. Enrique likes soccer.
Enrique plays every Saturday.

_____

6. The school offers a good program in business.
The school's recreational facilities are excellent.

_____

USING *ALSO* TO ADD INFORMATION

When two successive sentences introduce similar ideas, you can use the word *also* in the second sentence. *Also* usually goes before the main verb in the sentence, but it goes after the verb *be*. *Also* is a very useful word, but it shouldn't be used too often. Never use it in two successive sentences, and try to use it no more than twice in a paragraph.

Examples

Yara Haider likes Lebanon very much.
She <u>also</u> likes the students in her school.
Janet is in my English class.
She is <u>also</u> in my music class.

Use the caret symbol (^) when you edit to add something to a sentence.

Example

She is very pretty. She is ^very intelligent.
                                               also

_____

3 **Using *Also* in Sentences** Use a caret (^) to add *also* to the second sentence in each pair below.

1. David likes baseball. He ^likes rock music.
                                     also

2. Hamid is tall. He is very athletic.

3. In her free time, Maddie plays basketball. She likes to swim.

4. Efraim works part-time. He takes care of his four children.

4 **Writing Sentences with *And* and *Also*** Look at the notes from your interview. Write one sentence using *and* and one sentence using *also* to connect ideas.

_____

USING *BUT* AND *SO* TO CONNECT SENTENCES

You can also connect two sentences with *but* or *so*. Use a comma before these words when they connect two complete sentences.

But introduces contrasting information.

Examples
She thinks her English class is excellent.
She thinks the food in the cafeteria is terrible.
She thinks her English class is excellent, <u>but</u> she thinks the food in the cafeteria is terrible.

So introduces a result or an effect.

Examples
His company sells equipment to American hospitals.
He needs English for his work.
His company sells equipment to American hospitals, so he needs English for his work.

_____

5 **Using *And* and *But* to Connect Sentences** Connect the sentences below with *and* or *but*.

1. Alberto lives with his sister. She drives him to school every afternoon.

   Alberto lives with his sister, and she drives him to school every afternoon.

2. Yara can speak English well. She needs more writing practice.

   _____

   _____

3. Western Adult School is in a beautiful location. It doesn't have very good library facilities.

   _____

   _____

4. Yara is Syrian. She is studying in Lebanon.

   _____

   _____

5. Yara's father is proud of her. He's happy that she's studying in Lebanon.

   _____

   _____

6 **Using *But* and *So* to Connect Sentences** Connect the sentences below with *but* or *so*.

1. She has to work all day. She doesn't have time to do all of her homework.
   She has to work all day, so she doesn't have time to do all of her homework.

2. He likes his English class. He doesn't think the American students are very friendly.

   _____

   _____

3. Her company is opening an office in the United States. It needs English-speaking workers.

   _____

   _____

4. She likes academic life. She is homesick for her family.

   _____

   _____

5. Pedro wants to work in Japan. He needs to learn Japanese.

   _____

   _____

7 **Writing Sentences with *But* and *So*** Look at the notes from your interview. Write one sentence using *but* and one sentence using *so* to connect ideas.

Writing With Computers
When you write the first draft of your paragraph on a computer, set the line spacing to double space so you will have room to make notes and corrections later.

Strategy

Writing a First Draft
Good writers always write and then revise their work. The first time you write, you create the *first draft*. In the first draft, put your ideas together in the form of a paragraph. When you write the first draft, think about your ideas. Don't worry too much about grammar, spelling, or form.

ORDERING INFORMATION IN A PARAGRAPH

Information in a paragraph can be organized or ordered in many different ways. For your descriptive paragraph about a classmate, you will first write facts about the person you interviewed. Then you'll write about the person's opinions.

8 Writing the First Draft Write a paragraph about the person you interviewed. Remember to write about facts, then opinions. Use your graphic organizer and sentences you wrote earlier in the chapter. Don't worry about writing everything correctly in the first draft.

Part 3 Revising and Editing

Revising for Content and Editing for Form

Strategy

Revising for Content
You should review a piece of writing at least twice. The first time, you should revise it for content, and the second time, you should edit it for form.

When you revise your writing for content, focus on the ideas. Ask yourself if you have included everything you wanted to write about and if there are any unnecessary details. Also look at how ideas are connected and organized.

1 Revising for Content Look at the paragraph below. Focus only on the content—the writer's ideas and organization. Think about the following questions:

1. Does the paragraph have a good topic sentence?
2. Are all the sentences about one subject?
3. Is related information grouped together?
4. Can any sentences be connected? Which connecting words can you use?

Don't worry about misspelled words and other errors for now.

A New Class Member

This is about Wichai Tongkhio. is a new member of the English composition class at Amarin Community College. There many classes at ACC. he generally likes life in Bangkok. He likes the school. He doesn't like his dormitory. He is 18 years old. He is from a village in the north. He studying business administration, English and accounting. In his free time, he play basketball. He goes to movies. He plans to visit the United States next summer, so he needs to learn English.

Editing for Form

When you edit your writing for form, focus on the way the writing looks on the page, the grammar, spelling, and punctuation.

Here are some guidelines for forming paragraphs and sentences:

1. Write the title of your paragraph in the center of the first line.

2. Capitalize all important words in the title, but don't capitalize small words like *a*, *the*, *to*, *with*, and *at* unless they come at the beginning of the title.

3. Skip a line between the title and the paragraph, and indent (leave a space) at the beginning of the paragraph.

4. Begin every line except the first at the left margin (one inch from the edge of the paper).

5. Leave a one-inch margin on the right.

6. Use a period (.) or a question mark (?) at the end of every sentence. (For rules on punctuation, see Appendix 3.)

7. Leave one space after the period.

8. Begin every sentence with a capital letter. (For rules on capitalization, see Appendix 2.)

9. Capitalize names of people and places. (See Appendix 2.)

10. Use periods and commas only after words. Don't put them at the beginning of a new line.

11. Begin every sentence in a paragraph right after the sentence before it. Start on a new line only when you begin a new paragraph.

12. Don't write paragraphs with only one or two sentences. Most paragraphs have at least four or five sentences

---

2 **Editing for Form** Now edit the paragraph on page 13 again. This time, focus on form. Check the following:

1. The writer's use of third-person singular verbs in the present tense; they should end with -*s*.

2. The writer's use of negative verb forms, capitalization, and punctuation.

3. The writer's sentence and paragraph form.

4. Any other mistakes in form (use the guidelines above to help you).

Evaluating Your Writing

Strategy

Using Rubrics
A rubric is a set of characteristics you can use to evaluate your writing. To use the rubric, give your writing a score (3 = excellent, 2 = adequate, 1 = developing) for each characteristic.

3 **Using a Rubric** Read the rubric below with your class. Then use the rubric to score your paragraph.

Score	Description
3 **Excellent**	■ **Content:** Paragraph describes a classmate and includes facts about the person as well as her or his opinions. ■ **Organization:** Paragraph includes a topic sentence, introduces facts then opinions, and all sentences relate to the topic sentence. ■ **Vocabulary:** Vocabulary is clear, specific, varied, and used correctly throughout. ■ **Grammar:** Subjects and verbs agree, and singular and plural nouns are correct. *And*, *but*, *so*, and *also* are used correctly to connect ideas. ■ **Spelling and Mechanics:** Most words are spelled correctly, punctuation is correct, and paragraph form is followed.
2 **Adequate**	■ **Content:** Paragraph describes a classmate but may not include both facts and the person's opinions. ■ **Organization:** Paragraph includes a topic sentence, but one or two ideas in the paragraph may not connect to it. Ordering of some ideas may not be clear. ■ **Vocabulary:** Vocabulary is mostly clear and specific. One or two words may be used incorrectly. ■ **Grammar:** Subjects and verbs mostly agree, and singular and plural nouns are mostly correct. *And, but, so,* and *also* may be used incorrectly. ■ **Spelling and Mechanics:** Paragraph may include some spelling and/or punctuation mistakes. Correct paragraph form is mostly followed.

1 Developing	■ **Content**: Paragraph doesn't describe a classmate or may not include facts and opinions. ■ **Organization**: Topic sentence is unclear, incomplete, or absent, and ordering of ideas is unclear throughout. ■ **Vocabulary**: Vocabulary is limited or repeated, and/or there are too many mistakes to understand the ideas. ■ **Grammar**: Many subject and verb agreement mistakes and singular and plural noun mistakes. Many grammar mistakes make it difficult for the reader to understand the ideas. *And*, *but*, *so*, and *also* are not used or are used incorrectly throughout. ■ **Spelling and Mechanics**: Many distracting spelling and/or punctuation mistakes. Correct paragraph form is not followed.

PEER SHARING

Peer sharing is an important part of the writing process. When you're writing, it's hard to see your work from a reader's perspective. When someone else reads your writing and comments on it, he or she offers a different and fresh perspective. These thoughts and comments can help you in your revisions.

When you read your classmate's writing, read to get information, not to judge or correct the writing. Don't feel that you have to edit your peer's writing. When you finish reading your peer's work, first make positive comments. Mention the parts of the paragraph that you found most interesting or surprising. Then ask questions about sections that are confusing, or tell the writer where, as a reader, you want more information or detail.

4 **Peer Sharing** Read a classmate's paragraph. Did you learn anything new about the student he or she wrote about? If not, is there anything more that you would like to know?

5 **Writing the Second Draft**
Rewrite your paragraph using your rubric evaluation. Then give your paragraph to your teacher for comments and corrections. When your teacher returns your paper, ask him or her about any comments or corrections you don't understand.

▲ Peer sharing is an important part of the writing process.

1 Sharing Your Writing Share your paragraph with your classmates. Take turns reading the paragraphs aloud, or pass them around the room.

 2 Making a Class Newsletter Make a class newsletter with your paragraphs. Give the newsletter a title, and share it with other English classes.

 3 Interviewing Your Teacher As a class, interview your teacher. Write possible questions on the board. You can ask her or him these questions:

1. Where are you from?
2. What do you like to do in your free time?
3. What do you like about your job?

Strategy

Reading to Improve Your Writing
Did you know that reading improves your writing? As you read, you develop sentencing and paragraphing skills just by being exposed to good models. What you read is not important—anything you enjoy reading will help you.

4 Reading to Improve Your Writing Below are some ideas about reading for beginning students of English. Bring one item into class and share it with your peers.

1. Books written for beginning English language learners have easy English but adult topics. Ask your teacher if your school has any of these special readers you can borrow.
2. Books with pictures are easy to read. If you don't understand all the words, the pictures help. Comic books and children's books are excellent "picture books" for beginning students.
3. Supermarket newspapers (called *tabloids*) are fun and easy to read. Just don't believe everything you find in them. They often have stories—sometimes true, sometimes not—about crazy happenings and famous people in movies, TV, and sports.

What Do You Think?

Researching a Famous Person

Think of a famous person who inspires you: a politician, an athlete, or a movie or television star. Use a search engine to research this person on the Internet. Make a list of four websites you used to do your research. Answer the following questions:

▲ Joan Chen, actress

1. Where does the person live?

2. What is the person famous for?

3. How does the person spend his or her days?

4. What does the person like or dislike about his or her life and work?

5. What did you find out about his or her love life?

Analyzing Your Research In small groups, exchange paragraphs with your classmates. Discuss whether what you read is true. How do you know?

Strategy

Journal Writing

You can become a better writer by practicing often. For this reason, you are going to keep a journal in this class. Journal writing is a free-writing exercise. In free writing, you write quickly about what you are thinking or feeling. This is for practice, so *what* you are saying is more important than grammar and form. Each time you write something, what you write is called an *entry*. You can buy a special notebook for your journal entries, or you can write entries on separate pieces of paper and keep them in a folder. Sometimes you will have a time limit for free writing; sometimes you won't.

5 **Writing in Your Journal** For your first journal entry, write for 10 minutes about yourself. Write about how you are feeling, what you are doing, or what you think of your school or your English class. If you want to, you can show your entry to your teacher or a classmate.

Self-Assessment Log

In this chapter, you worked through the following activities. How much did they help you become a better writer? Check *A lot*, *A little*, or *Not at all*.

	A lot	A little	Not at all
I interviewed a classmate.	❏	❏	❏
I distinguished fact from opinion.	❏	❏	❏
I created a graphic organizer.	❏	❏	❏
I learned about topic sentences.	❏	❏	❏
I connected ideas with *and, but,* and *so.*	❏	❏	❏
I used *also* to add information.	❏	❏	❏
I learned to revise for content and edit for form.	❏	❏	❏
I used a writing rubric to evaluate my first draft.	❏	❏	❏
(Add something) _____	❏	❏	❏

_____

2

Experiencing Nature

In This Chapter

Genre Focus: Descriptive

Writing Product

A descriptive paragraph about a painting

Writing Process

- Analyze and discuss paintings.
- Order information from general to specific.
- Group details in spatial order.
- Use descriptive adjectives.
- Use prepositional phrases.
- Use the present continuous.
- Use pronouns and articles.

❝ In all things of nature there is something of the marvelous. **❞**

—Aristotle
Greek philosopher (384 BC—322 BC)

Connecting to the Topic

1. Have you ever seen a scene like this? If so, where?

2. What kinds of animals would you expect to find here?

3. What are some adjectives that would describe this place?

Exploring Ideas

1 **Analyzing a Painting** In small groups, use the following questions to discuss the painting below:

1. What is the title of the painting?
2. What is a shark?
3. Which man is Watson? Why do you think he is naked?
4. How many people are in the picture?
5. What is happening in the picture?
6. How does the picture make you feel?
7. What can you see in the background? Where do you think this is happening?

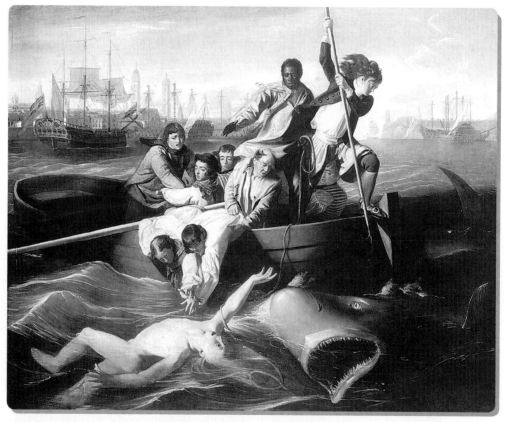

▲ *Watson and the Shark*, John Singleton Copley, U.S., 1738–1815. Oil on canvas; 72 × 90 1/4 in. (182 × 229.2 cm). Gift of Mrs. George von Lengerke Meyer. Courtesy, Museum of Fine Arts, Boston. Reproduced with permission. © 2000 Museum of Fine Arts, Boston. All Rights Reserved.

Building Vocabulary

2 **Using a Vocabulary Chart** In this chapter, you are going to write a descriptive paragraph about *Watson and the Shark*. Think about the vocabulary you will need to write your paragraph. What new vocabulary did you use in Activity 1? Add your words to the chart.

Nouns	Adjectives	Verbs	Other
background	afraid	attack	
harbor	dark	hold	
oar	dramatic	kill	
rope	frightening	reach	
rowboat	huge	rescue	
shark	naked	try	
ship			
spear			
teeth			

3 **Using New Vocabulary** Join a group of three students and do the following with the words in the chart and the painting *Watson and the Shark*:

1. Point to an example of each noun in the painting.

2. Point to one person or thing in the painting that can be described with each adjective in the chart.

3. For each verb in the chart, point to one person or thing in the painting that could go with that verb. Example: (verb) *reach,* point to the man in the painting who is reaching.

4 **Writing with New Vocabulary** Write four sentences about the picture using as many of the vocabulary words in the chart as you can. Underline the words you used from the chart and count them. Which student in the class used the most words from his or her chart?

_____

_____

_____

_____

_____

5 **Generating New Vocabulary through Discussion** What do you know about sharks? Make a note of words that may be useful for your writing as you discuss the questions below in small groups. Then read the information in the boxes that follow.

1. Are there many sharks where you come from?

2. If so, are they dangerous?

3. What do you know about shark attacks?

4. How many people do you think sharks kill every year?

More About *Watson and the Shark*

The scene in *Watson and the Shark* really happened. Mr. Brook Watson was swimming in the Havana harbor in Cuba when the shark attacked. The shark bit his leg, but Mr. Watson did not die. He was a politician, and he wanted to get publicity, so he asked the American painter John Singleton Copley (1738–1815) to paint the scene. Watson later became Lord Mayor of London.

More About Sharks

No one knows for sure where the English word *shark* comes from. Some people think it is from the Mayan Indian word *xoc*, meaning "shark." Others think it is from the German *schurke*, meaning "a bad person." In English, *shark* can also mean a dishonest person or someone who is very aggressive. It is sometimes used in a business context. People all over the world are afraid of sharks. But sharks are not very dangerous—they only kill about 25 people every year.

Organizing Ideas

Strategy

Ordering Information in a Paragraph
Descriptive paragraphs often begin with general information—information that describes the whole subject. Then the writer adds specific information—information that describes the details of the subject. This is called *moving from general to specific.* The details support the general statements.

6 Distinguishing General and Specific Information Read the paragraph below, which describes the painting *A Sunday on La Grande Jatte*. Which sentences give general information? Which sentences give specific information?

▲ George Seurat, French, 1859–1891, *A Sunday on La Grande Jatte*, 1848; oil on canvas, 1884–1886, 207.5 × 308 cm, Helen Birch Bartlett Memorial Collection, 1926.224. Photograph © 1994, The Art Institute of Chicago. All Rights Reserved.

A Sunday on La Grande Jatte by George Seurat is a picture of a Parisian park on a warm and sunny day. Although the scene is quite busy, it also seems quiet and peaceful. On the left, there is a lake. Three sailboats are moving on the lake. Four men and one woman are riding in a canoe. On the shore, some people are lying on the grass gazing at the water. In the background, a man is playing a trumpet. Two soldiers are standing motionless. On the right, a man and a woman are dressed in elegant clothes. They are staring at the water. There is a monkey dancing at their feet. In the center, a woman is holding an umbrella with one hand and a little girl with the other.

7 Identifying the Topic Sentence Underline the topic sentence in the paragraph above. Remember that the topic sentence is the most general statement in the paragraph. It introduces the main idea, but it doesn't give any details.

8 **Choosing the Best Topic Sentence** Look at the painting, *Watson and the Shark* on page 22 again. Which of the following sentences would make a good topic sentence for a paragraph about the painting?

1. *Watson and the Shark* is a good painting.

2. In this painting, there are some men in a boat.

3. The men in this painting are afraid.

4. *Watson and the Shark,* by John Singleton Copley, shows a dramatic rescue attempt.

5. John Singleton Copley painted *Watson and the Shark* in 1778.

9 **Writing General Statements** Below is a general statement about *Watson and the Shark*. Add two more general statements about the painting.

1. *It is a horrific scene in which a young man is being attacked by a ferocious shark.*

2. _____

   _____

3. _____

   _____

10 **Writing About Details** Below are two details of the painting that you should mention in your description. Write a sentence about each, and add two more sentences about two other details of the painting.

the rowboat
the sea

_____

_____

_____

_____

_____

_____

11 **Ordering Ideas in a Paragraph** Number the sentences in Activity 10 in the order that you would use them in your paragraph. Try to put them in spatial order. That is, group the details of the painting that are near each other.

Part 2 | Developing Writing Skills

Developing Cohesion and Clarity

USING ADJECTIVES TO WRITE ABOUT DETAILS

An adjective is a word that describes a noun. Colors are adjectives. Words such as *tall*, *thin*, *curly*, *hungry*, *round*, *happy*, and *sick* are adjectives too. Adjectives make descriptive writing more interesting. They can be in two different positions:

1. After verbs such as *be*, *seem*, *look*, *feel*, and *get*

Examples
The men are <u>young</u>.
The men look <u>horrified</u>.
The boy feels <u>terrified</u>.
The shark is getting <u>hungry</u>.

Note: If you want to use more than one adjective, you can connect them with *and*.

Example
The shark is huge <u>and</u> frightening.

2. Before a noun

Example
The <u>young</u> men are in a <u>tiny</u> boat.

---

 1 Listing Adjectives Look at *Watson and the Shark* on page 22 again. With a partner, make a list of adjectives to describe the following nouns. Use your imagination for the colors.

1. the boat.
small, overloaded

2. the men in the boat

3. the weather

4. the shark

5. the man in the water

6. the water

2 **Using Adjectives in Sentences** Write five sentences using the phrases and adjectives you wrote in Activity 1.

1. *The small, overloaded boat looks like it's going to sink.*

2. _____

3. _____

4. _____

5. _____

6. _____

USING PREPOSITIONAL PHRASES TO WRITE ABOUT DETAILS

Prepositions are words such as *on*, *in*, *toward*, *during*, and *with*. They give information about location, direction, and time. A preposition followed by a noun is called a prepositional phrase.

Examples

preposition	+	**noun**
on		the table
near		the door

Prepositions of location will be the most useful for your paragraph. Some common prepositions and prepositional phrases of location are:

above	**in**	**next to**
at	**in front of**	**on**
behind	**in the middle of**	**under**
beside	**near**	

You can put prepositional phrases at the beginning, in the middle, or at the end of sentences.

Examples

<u>In the park</u>, there are many large trees.
Many large trees <u>in the park</u> are several hundred years old.
There are people <u>in the park</u>.

3 **Identifying Prepositional Phrases of Location** Look at the paragraph about the Seurat painting on page 25. Underline all of the prepositional phrases that show location.

4 **Adding Prepositional Phrases to Sentences** The sentences below describe the metalwork, *The Tree of Life*, by the Haitian artist, Georges Liautaud. Add one of the prepositional phrases from the box to each of the sentences.

▲ *The Tree of Life* by Georges Liautaud. Sculpture from the collection of Selden Rodman. Photo by Selden Rodman.

at a table	under the tree of life
to the left	out of the tree
to the right	in the center

1. _In the center_ _____ is the tree of life.

2. Two children are standing _____ .

3. Several birds are flying _____ .

4. On the right are two people sitting _____ .

5. _____ a man, a woman, and a baby are in a boat.

6. _____ is a smaller tree.

5 **Writing Sentences with Prepositional Phrases** Write three more sentences about *The Tree of Life* using prepositional phrases.

1. _____

2. _____

3. _____

6 **Writing Sentences with Prepositions of Location** Look at the painting
Watson and the Shark on page 22 again. Write five sentences about details using
prepositions of location.

USING PRONOUNS

You can use pronouns to replace nouns in your writing when what the pronoun refers
to is clear. Pronouns add variety to your writing and help to connect your ideas. Below
are some examples of subject and object pronouns.

	Singular	Plural	Examples	Notes
Subject Pronouns	I you he, she, it	we you they	Seurat was a French painter. *He* is famous today.	*He* and *him* both refer to Seurat.
Object Pronouns	me you him, her, it	us you them	I studied *him* in art history.	

7 **Identifying Pronouns** Circle all the pronouns in the paragraph about Seurat's
painting on page 25. Then draw an arrow from each pronoun to the noun it represents
or refers to.

8 **Changing Nouns to Pronouns** Read
theparagraph on page 31 about the painting
Snow Hill and Drum Bridge at Meguro. Change
some of the nouns to pronouns. Then compare
your new paragraph with a classmate's.

▲ *"Drum Bridge and Sunset Hill, Meguro,
from the series, One Hundred Famous
Views of Edo, Number 111, 1857", by
Ichiryusai Hiroshige (Japanese, 1797-
1858), Wood-block print on paper, Gibbes
Museum of Art/Carolina Art Association*

The painting *Snow Hill and Drum Bridge at Meguro* is by Hiroshige. Hiroshige painted *Snow Hill and Drum Bridge at Meguro* in 1857. *Snow Hill and Drum Bridge at Meguro* is a winter scene. In the middle of the painting, there is a stone bridge over a small river. Although it is winter, the water in the river isn't frozen. The water is flowing peacefully. There are several people on the bridge. The people are walking through the deep snow. Some of the people are carrying heavy loads. There are also many trees in the painting. The trees are white because the trees are covered in snow. In the picture, it is nighttime. The night is cloudless and many stars are shining in the sky. I like this painting because the scene is calm and quiet.

USING THE PRESENT CONTINUOUS

You can use the present continuous form of a verb to describe what is happening in a picture. Present continuous verbs have two parts:

> the verb *be* (*is, are*) + verb + *ing*

Examples
Watson <u>is swimming</u> near the shark.
The men <u>are trying</u> to help Watson.

9 **Identifying the Present Continuous** Read the paragraph about *Snow Hill and Drum Bridge at Meguro* above, and underline four examples of the present continuous.

SPELLING RULES FOR ADDING –*ING* TO A VERB

1. If the simple form of the verb ends in a silent -*e* after a consonant, drop the -*e* and add -*ing*.

   Examples
   race/racing   move/moving

2. If the simple form ends in -*ie*, change the -*ie* to *y* and add -*ing*.

   Examples
   die/dying   untie/untying

3. If the simple form is one syllable and ends in one consonant after one vowel, double the last consonant (except *x*) and add -*ing*.

   Examples
   run/running   get/getting

Note that *w* and *y* at the end of words are vowels, not consonants.

4. If the simple form ends in a stressed syllable, follow rule number 3.

   Examples

   begin/beginning

5. If the last syllable is not stressed, just add *-ing*.

   Examples

   happen/happening

6. In all other cases, add *-ing* to the simple form.

---

10 **Writing the *-ing* Form of Verbs** Write the *-ing* form of the verbs below. Use the spelling rules above to help you.

1. swim   *swimming*

2. stare   _____

3. try   _____

4. throw   _____

5. stand   _____

6. attack   _____

7. look   _____

8. bite   _____

9. see   _____

10. refer   _____

USING ARTICLES: *A, AN,* AND *THE*

A, an, and *the* are articles and introduce nouns. *A* and *an* are indefinite articles. They describe general nouns. *The* is a definite article. It describes specific nouns.

	Examples	Notes
Indefinite Articles	**A:** I can drive a car, but I can't fly <u>an</u> airplane. **B:** Really? I can do both.	The speakers are talking about cars and airplanes in general—any cars or airplanes.
Definite Articles	**C:** Are you finished writing <u>the</u> reports yet? **D:** Not yet. Do you want to use <u>the</u> computer? **C:** That's all right. I can wait.	The speakers are talking about specific reports and a specific computer. Both speakers know which reports and which computers they are talking about.
	Look at <u>the</u> sun. It looks red.	There is only one sun, so we always refer to it with the definite article, *the*.

Usually *a* or *an* comes before a noun when the noun appears for the first time. After that, *the* appears before the noun.

Examples	Notes
This is <u>a</u> painting of <u>an</u> island near Paris.	In the first sentence, the painting and the island are being introduced or mentioned for the first time. *A* and *an* are used.
<u>The</u> painting is very famous, and so is <u>the</u> island.	In the second sentence, the painting and the island are mentioned again, and now it is clear which painting and which island the speaker is referring to. *The* is used.

11 **Adding Articles to Sentences** Complete the sentences in the following paragraph about *The Tree of Life* with *a*, *an*, or *the*.

There is ___*a*___ large tree in the middle. Two children are standing
under _____ tree, and two children are climbing in _____ tree. _____ children are waving. On the left is _____ man and _____ woman in _____ boat.
_____ man is fishing. _____ woman is holding _____ child. _____ large bird
is flying over _____ boat. To the right is _____ smaller tree. Two people
are sitting under _____ tree at _____ table. On _____ table is _____ plant.

12 **Writing the First Draft** Write a descriptive paragraph about the painting, *Watson and the Shark* on page 22. Remember to:

- start with general statements, and then add details.
- group details in spatial order.
- use the present continuous to tell what is happening.
- write the first draft without worrying about making mistakes in form and grammar.

Revising for Content and Editing for Form

1 **Revising for Content** Revise the paragraph below for content. Ask yourself the following questions:

1. Does the paragraph describe all of the important elements of the painting, *The Starry Night*?

2. Do the statements move from general to specific?

3. Does the author make good use of adjectives and describe the painting accurately?

Don't worry about misspelled words and other errors for now.

The Starry Night is the painting by Vincent van Gogh, a Dutch artist. There are some houses and buildings around a church. In the front of the painting are some tall, curving trees, and in the back are some rolling mountains. Our eyes follow their shapes up, around, down, and back again, like a ride on a roller coaster. In the center is a church. The stars, trees, and mountains look like they are moving. It is the beautiful scene of a sky full of bright stars.

◄ Vincent van Gogh. *The Starry Night* (1889). Oil on canvas, 29 × 361/4 in. The Museum of Modern Art, New York. Acquired through the Lillie P. Bliss Bequest. Photograph © 1995, The Museum of Modern Art, New York.

2 **Editing for Form** Edit the paragraph on page 34 for form. Check it for correct use of *a*, *an*, and *the*. Does the paragraph follow the rules for correct form? Use the guidelines on page 14 to help you. Make any other changes you think are necessary.

Evaluating Your Writing

3 **Using a Rubric** Read the rubric below with your class. Then use the rubric to score your paragraph.

Score	Description
3 **Excellent**	■ **Content:** Paragraph includes enough information about the painting so that the reader can imagine it. ■ **Organization:** Paragraph includes a topic sentence and ideas that move from general to specific. All sentences connect to the topic sentence. Spatially related details are grouped together. ■ **Vocabulary:** Vocabulary is specific enough so that the reader has a very clear understanding of the painting. Varied and vivid adjectives are used. ■ **Grammar:** Articles, prepositional phrases, pronouns, and the present continuous are used correctly. There are very few grammar problems, and the description of the painting is clear. ■ **Spelling and Mechanics:** Most words are spelled correctly, punctuation is correct, and paragraph form is followed.
2 **Adequate**	■ **Content:** Paragraph includes information about the painting, but details may be limited, or the reader may have questions. ■ **Organization:** Paragraph includes a topic sentence, but some related details are not grouped together or may not connect to the topic. General and specific ideas may be mixed up. All spatially related details may not be grouped together. ■ **Vocabulary:** Vocabulary is mostly clear and correct. Use of adjectives may be limited. ■ **Grammar:** Articles, prepositional phrases, pronouns, and the present continuous are mostly used correctly. There are a few grammar problems, but the reader can understand the ideas. ■ **Spelling and Mechanics:** There are some spelling and/or punctuation mistakes and/or problems with form.

1 **Developing**	■ **Content:** Paragraph does not include much information about the painting, or it presents too many unrelated details. ■ **Organization:** Paragraph ideas do not connect to the topic sentence, or there is no topic sentence. The order of information is confusing. ■ **Vocabulary:** Vocabulary is limited, and/or there are too many mistakes to understand the ideas. Few adjectives are used. ■ **Grammar:** Many problems with articles, prepositional phrases, pronouns, and the present continuous. Grammar mistakes make it difficult for the reader to understand the ideas. ■ **Spelling and Mechanics:** Many distracting spelling and/or punctuation mistakes. Correct paragraph form is not used.

 4 **Peer Sharing** Show your paragraph to another student. Compare your descriptions. How are they the same? How are they different?

5 **Writing the Second Draft** Rewrite your paragraph using your rubric evaluation. Then give your paragraph to your teacher for comments and corrections. When your teacher returns your paragraph, compare it to your paragraph from Chapter 1. Answer the following questions:

1. In what ways is your writing improving?

2. What things do you still need to work on?

Writing with Computers

Always read your work again after you have made changes. Make sure you have not forgotten to remove old text. For example, if you change the sentence, "Writing in English is not an easy thing." to "Writing in English is not easy." you may end up with "Writing in English is not an easy." This sentence is not correct.

What Do You Think?

Analyzing Paintings Look at the different kinds of art shown throughout this chapter. Discuss the following questions as a class:

1. What do the Rivera mural on page 37 and *Watson and the Shark* both show?

2. Which two pieces of art are the most different? Why?

3. Which two pieces of art are the most similar? Why?

4. Which art do you like? Why?

5. Which art don't you like? Why?

▲ Diego Rivera. *La lluvia* (Rain). Mural, 2.05 × 2.284 m. Court of Fiestas, level 3, West Wall. Painted ca. July 1923–early 1924, Secretaria de Education Publica, Mexico City, Mexico. Schalkwijk–Art Resource, NY.

Part 4 | Expansion Activities

1 **Writing About Scenery** Find a picture or a photo of a scene that you like. Write a descriptive paragraph about it. Use general and specific statements, and include a sentence about how the picture makes you feel.

2 **Matching the Picture to the Paragraph** Your teacher will collect your pictures from Activity 1 and put them in the front of the room. Then you and your classmates will read your descriptions to the class. The class will guess which picture each student is describing.

3 **Making a Travel Brochure** Make a travel brochure about a place you like and know well. Bring in pictures of the place if you can. Next to the pictures, write a paragraph answering the following questions:

1. What's the name of the place?
2. Where is it?
3. What's the easiest way to get there?
4. Why should tourists visit there?
5. What will they like?
6. What interesting, beautiful, or historical sights are there to see?

4 **Writing in Your Journal** Choose one of the following activities:

1. Sit in a park, an outdoor café, or another place where you can observe, and describe the scene around you. Write about what you see. Are there people? What are they doing? Do they look happy, sad, or bored? How is the weather? Is it cloudy, sunny, or windy?

2. Describe your home. Where is it? What is in it? Do you like your home? Why or why not?

 5 **Researching a Painting** Use a search engine to do research on the Internet about one of the paintings in this chapter or any other painting that interests you. Find out the following information:

1. Where is/was the painter from?
2. What style of art is the painting?
3. How much did the painting cost the last time it was sold?
4. What inspired the artist to create this work?

Find an article about the painting and read it. Notice the adjectives the writer uses to describe the painting. Are they the same ones you used? Write down and look up any new vocabulary you come across.

Self-Assessment Log

In this chapter, you worked through the following activities. How much did they help you become a better writer? Check *A lot*, *A little*, or *Not at all*.

	A lot	A little	Not at all
I analyzed and discussed paintings.	❑	❑	❑
I ordered information from general to specific.	❑	❑	❑
I learned to group details in spatial order.	❑	❑	❑
I learned to use descriptive adjectives.	❑	❑	❑
I practiced using prepositions of place.	❑	❑	❑
I used the present continuous to describe a painting.	❑	❑	❑
I practiced using pronouns and articles.	❑	❑	❑
I used a writing rubric to evaluate my first draft.	❑	❑	❑
(Add something) _____	❑	❑	❑

_____

Living to Eat or Eating to Live?

❝ Tell me what you eat, and I will tell you what you are. **❞**

—Anthelme Brillat-Savarin
French politician and food writer (1755–1826)

Connecting to the Topic

1 Do you recognize these foods? How many can you name?

2 Have you ever eaten these foods? If so, which ones?

3 What is your favorite dish?

Exploring Ideas

 1 **Describing Holiday Foods** Discuss the picture below with a partner. What are the people doing? Do you think they are celebrating something? What?

2 **Free Writing** Write in your journal about typical everyday meals that you eat. Write as much as you can in about 5 minutes. Don't worry about form or grammar.

 3 **Discussing Your Free Write** Join a group of three students and discuss your journal entries. Make a list of the different kinds of food from the discussion. Write a description for each one.

Food	Description
tacos	*corn pancakes with meat and salad*
_____	_____
_____	_____
_____	_____
_____	_____

Culture Note

Thanksgiving

Thanksgiving is an important American holiday celebrated each year on the fourth Thursday in November. On this day, Americans give thanks for everything that they have. They eat a big meal with many special foods such as turkey, stuffing, sweet potatoes, pumpkin pie, and cranberry sauce.

4 **Writing About a Holiday** Think of a holiday that you celebrate, and write it below. Then list some of the foods that you eat on that holiday, and describe the foods. If there is no English word for certain foods, write them in your first language.

Your holiday: _____

Foods that you eat: _____

_____

_____

_____

5 **Comparing Holiday Foods with Regular Food** Write three sentences that compare the special food you eat on holidays with the food you eat every day.

Example

The Thanksgiving meal is more delicious than our everyday meals
and requires much more preparation.

▲ A traditional Thanksgiving dinner

Building Vocabulary

6 **Using a Vocabulary Chart** Write the underlined words in the following sentences in the correct columns of the chart below.

1. Stuffing is a <u>mixture</u> of bread and spices.

2. Spring rolls are a Chinese <u>specialty</u>.

3. The Chinese <u>celebrate</u> New Year's in February.

4. On Thanksgiving, Americans <u>traditionally</u> feast on turkey and stuffing.

5. To prepare tabouleh, we <u>mix</u> parsley, mint, tomatoes, and bulgar (wheat).

6. People often eat <u>special</u> foods at celebrations.

7. Every country has <u>traditional</u> foods.

8. I enjoy family holidays, <u>especially</u> Thanksgiving.

Nouns	Verbs	Adjectives	Other
mixture			

 7 **Adding Words to the Vocabulary Chart** Work in small groups. Share the sentences you wrote in Activity 5. What vocabulary is new to you? Add new words to the chart above.

 8 **Generating New Vocabulary Through Discussion** In small groups, discuss the foods you listed in Activities 3 and 4. Answer the questions below. Make a note of words that may be useful for your writing.

1. Which foods contain vegetables?

2. Which foods are sweet?

3. Which foods contain meat?

4. Which foods do you eat cold? hot?

Organizing Ideas

ORDERING INFORMATION IN A PARAGRAPH

A descriptive paragraph often begins with general statements then moves to more specific ones. The last sentence of a descriptive paragraph is often a personal opinion or idea.

Example

topic sentence: most general statement

general statement (more specific than the topic sentence)

specific statement, including details

Thanksgiving is a family celebration to remember the American colonists. Americans eat many traditional foods at Thanksgiving. Some typical Thanksgiving foods are turkey, stuffing, sweet potatoes, homemade bread, and pies. People eat more than usual on Thanksgiving, but they feel full and happy.

personal opinion/idea

---

9 **Ordering Ideas in a Paragraph** Organize the following sentences into the correct order to make a descriptive paragraph. Number them from 1, for the first, to 5, for the last.

1. _____ It is a day for families to celebrate together.

2. _____ For this meal, most families eat many traditional foods such as turkey, sweet potatoes, and cranberry sauce.

3. _____ Everyone eats more than usual, and at the end of the day, we are as stuffed (full) as the turkey.

4. _1_ On Thanksgiving Day, Americans remember the first Thanksgiving feast of the early American colonists.

5. _____ The most important activity on this day is Thanksgiving dinner.

10 **Analyzing a Graphic Organizer** As a class, discuss the information in the graphic organizer below. Answer the following questions:

1. How does the information in the rectangles relate to the information in the squares?

2. How does the information in the ovals relate to the information in the rectangles?

3. How does the information in the triangles relate to the information in the oval?

4. Can you think of any other information to add? Where would it go?

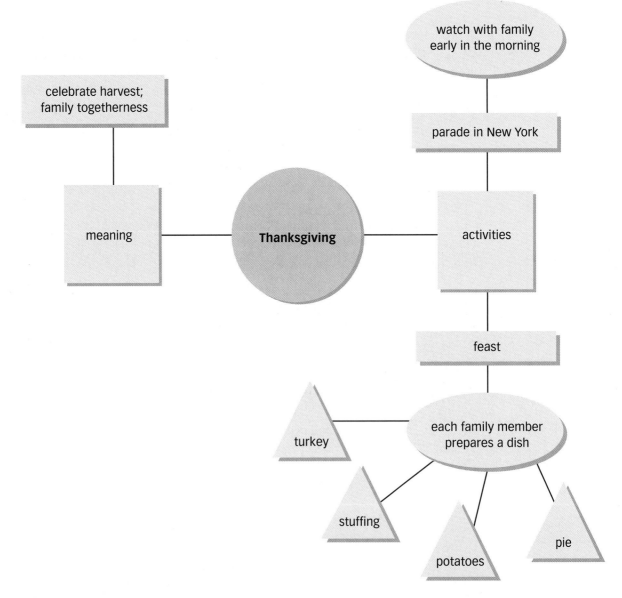

11 Creating a Graphic Organizer Brainstorm ideas about a holiday, and organize the ideas in a graphic organizer. Use the graphic organizer on page 46 as a model. Use the following questions to get you started:

1. What is the name of the holiday?

2. What do you celebrate on the holiday?

3. What do you do on the holiday?

4. What does your family eat on the holiday?

5. How do you feel about the holiday meal?

Writing Topic Sentences

Strategy

The Topic Sentence
Remember that the topic sentence:
- gives the main idea of the paragraph.
- is the most general statement in the paragraph.
- is often the first sentence in a paragraph, but it may come later.

12 Choosing the Best Topic Sentence Look at the sentences about the Thanksgiving meal in Activity 9 on page 45. Which sentence is the topic sentence? Underline it.

 13 Writing a Draft Topic Sentence Look at the graphic organizer you created for your paragraph. Write a draft topic sentence for your paragraph. Exchange your organizer and topic sentence with a partner and answer the following questions:

1. Does your partner's graphic organizer contain enough information to write an interesting paragraph? If not, what information is missing?

2. Is the information organized well?

3. Does the topic sentence give the main idea? Is it general enough?

Developing Cohesion and Clarity

COUNT AND NONCOUNT NOUNS

There are two kinds of nouns in English: count and noncount nouns. Look at the examples in the chart below.

	Examples		Notes
	Singular	**Plural**	
Count Nouns	a dish an ingredient a chickpea a turkey* one potato	three dishes two ingredients some chickpeas many turkeys a lot of potatoes	Singular count nouns often have *a*, *an*, or *one* before them. Plural count nouns can have numbers or other expressions of quantity† before them. Most plural count nouns have *-s* or *-es* endings.
Noncount Nouns	rice juice tahini a lot of turkey* some salt a little sugar sweetness		Noncount nouns name things, such as materials, liquids, and qualities, such as *sweetness*. Noncount nouns do not have clear boundaries and cannot be counted. You can use some expressions of quantity before noncount nouns, but you can't use *a*, *an*, or numbers.† Noncount nouns have no plural forms.

* Some nouns can be used as count or noncount nouns. For example:

  How many <u>turkeys</u> are you going to buy? (count)

  I love to eat <u>turkey</u> on Thanksgiving. (noncount)

† Some expressions of quantity are *some*, *a few*, *a lot of*, *a little*, and *many*.

1 **Distinguishing Count and Noncount Nouns** Look at the list of foods you created in Activity 4 on page 43. Work in a small group. Write *N* after the noncount nouns and *C* after the count nouns. If a word can be both count and noncount, write *NC*. If you are not sure about a word, use a dictionary.

2 Categorizing Foods Look at the following list of dishes from around the world. In small groups, discuss what the different dishes are. Then write the name of each dish under the correct heading in the chart below.

baklava	fried rice	saag
chow mein	hummus	samosas
curry	kufta kabob	spring rolls
dim sum	paneer	tabouleh

Chinese	Middle Eastern	Indian
fried rice		

GIVING EXAMPLES WITH *SUCH AS*

When you write, you can introduce examples with the phrase, *such as*.

Example

On Thanksgiving Day, we eat many traditional foods. We eat turkey, sweet potatoes, and cranberries.

On Thanksgiving Day, we eat many traditional foods <u>such as</u> turkey, sweet potatoes, and cranberries.

3 Writing Sentences with *Such As* Use the information in the chart above to write sentences with *such as* on the lines below.

1. Chinese restaurants serve many wonderful dishes <u>*such as fried rice,*</u>
   <u>*dumplings, and spring rolls.*</u>

2. In Chinese restaurants you, can try delicious dishes _____
   _____
   _____

3. _____
   _____
   _____

4 **Writing Sentences with *Such As*.** Look at your list of nouns from Activity 6 on page 44. Write three sentences with *such as* using some of the nouns on the list. Share your sentences with a classmate.

Example

On Thanksgiving Americans eat special dishes such as turkey and stuffing.

1. _____

_____

_____

2. _____

_____

_____

3. _____

_____

_____

USING APPOSITIVES

In writing about food, you have to explain what some dishes are. You can use appositives to do this effectively. An appositive is a word or phrase that modifies a noun or a noun phrase and follows it directly. It is separated from the rest of the sentence by commas.

Examples

Stuffing is a traditional Thanksgiving food. Stuffing is a mixture of bread and spices.

Stuffing, <u>a mixture of bread and spices,</u> is a traditional Thanksgiving food.

We fill the turkey with stuffing. Stuffing is a mixture of bread and spices.

We fill the turkey with stuffing, <u>a mixture of bread and spices</u>.

5 **Combining Sentences with Appositives** Use appositives to combine the following sentences:

1. A typical Middle Eastern dish is falafel. Falafel is a mixture of fried chickpeas and spices.

   A typical Middle Eastern dish is falafel, a mixture of fried chickpeas

   and spices.

2. We like to eat fajitas. Fajitas are slices of chicken or beef wrapped in a tortilla with fried peppers and onions.

   _____

   _____

3. My grandmother is famous for her tempura. Tempura is a traditional Japanese preparation of shellfish and vegetables.

_____

_____

4. A favorite Iranian dish is fesenjan. Fesenjan is chicken in a spicy pomegranate sauce.

_____

_____

6 **Writing Sentences with Appositives** Write four sentences that describe foods served on the holiday you are going to write about. Use appositives. Then share your sentences with another student.

Example _A popular Thanksgiving dish in my household is garlic mashed potatoes, a big bowl of mashed potatoes mixed with garlic, cream, and butter._

1. _____

_____

2. _____

_____

3. _____

_____

4. _____

_____

7 **Writing the First Draft** Write your descriptive paragraph about holiday foods. Include the name of the holiday in your title. Use your topic sentence and graphic organizer to develop and organize your paragraph. Use _such as_ and appositives in your paragraph.

▲ Typical foods eaten at Fourth of July celebrations

Revising for Content and Editing for Form

1 **Revising for Content** Review the paragraph below for content. Find a place to use *such as* before examples. Then find a place to combine two sentences using an appositive. Don't worry about misspelled words and other errors for now.

Special Christmas Foods

Christmas is an important holiday for many people. People in North America prepares many special Christmas foods from all over the world. Many Christmas specialties come from Great Britain. Fruitcake and eggnog come from Great Britain. North Americans make fruitcaks with fruites nuts and liquors. Eggnog is a drink of eggs, milk, and sometimes rum. Eggnog is a very creamy and delicious drink. Americans also eat a lot of Christmas cookies. I love the many special Christmas foods.

▲ An assortment of Christmas cookies

EDITING FOR FORM: USING COMMAS IN LISTS
We use commas to separate three or more items in a list. The items in the list may be nouns, adjectives, verbs, or phrases.

Nouns
We eat <u>turkey</u>, <u>stuffing</u>, and <u>fruit pies</u> on Thanksgiving.
We spend a long time <u>cooking</u>, <u>eating</u>, and <u>washing up</u>.

Adjectives
On Thanksgiving, my home is always <u>noisier</u>, <u>warmer</u>, and more <u>fragrant</u> than on other days of the year.

Verbs
I <u>got up</u>, <u>got dressed</u>, and <u>started cooking</u>.

Phrases
On Thanksgiving, my family enjoys *<u>cooking together,</u> <u>eating a huge meal,</u>* and *<u>watching our favorite teams play football on television</u>*.

---

2 **Adding Commas** The sentences below include appositives and lists, but the commas are missing. Add the commas.

1. Subs, large sandwiches filled with meat, cheese, and vegetables, are popular in the United States.
2. Americans often eat hot dogs pork or beef sausages on the Fourth of July.
3. Thais love to eat foods with different tastes such as hot sour sweet and spicy.
4. For lunch I often have tabouleh a Middle Eastern salad made from parsley mint tomatoes and wheat.
5. The Italian restaurant near my house serves pasta pizza and delicious minestrone soup.
6. Spaghetti an Italian noodle dish is popular in North America.

3 **Forming Plural Nouns** Write the correct plural forms of the following nouns. (See Appendix 1 for spelling rules).

cookie	_cookies_	dish	_____
orange	_____	tomato	_____
dish	_____	knife	_____
pancake	_____	serving	_____
cherry	_____	box	_____

Writing With Computers

Checking your Spelling

Most software programs have a tool that checks your spelling. However, the spell-check tool will not mark a misused word. In other words, if you write, **There books are here**, a spell-check tool will not mark **there** as incorrect because **there** is a word; it is just used incorrectly here. Therefore, you should edit your writing for spelling mistakes in addition to using the spell-check tool.

4 **Spelling Third-Person Singular Verbs** Write the correct third-person singular forms of the verbs in parentheses. (See Appendix 1, for spelling rules.)

He (miss)	_misses_	She (hurry)	_____
She (watch)	_____	It (wash)	_____
He (cook)	_____	He (drink)	_____
It (eat)	_____	She (dry)	_____

5 **Editing for Form** Edit the paragraph on page 52 for form. Make corrections in punctuation and spelling.

Evaluating Your Writing

6 **Using a Rubric** Read the rubric below with your class. Then use the rubric to score your paragraph.

Score	Description
3 **Excellent**	■ **Content:** Paragraph presents enough information about a holiday and its foods so that the reader has a clear idea of both. ■ **Organization:** Paragraph has a topic sentence. All sentences connect to this topic and move smoothly from general to specific. Related details are grouped together. Appositives and *such as* are used to add detail. ■ **Vocabulary:** Words are specific, varied, and used correctly throughout. ■ **Grammar:** Present tense verbs, count and noncount nouns, and appositives are used correctly throughout. ■ **Spelling and Mechanics:** Most words are spelled correctly, and commas are used correctly.
2 **Adequate**	■ **Content:** Paragraph presents information about a holiday and its food, but it may be short or the reader may have questions. ■ **Organization:** Paragraph includes a topic sentence, but some related details are not grouped together or may not connect to the topic. Ideas may not move from general to specific. ■ **Vocabulary:** Words are mostly specific, varied, and used correctly. ■ **Grammar:** Present tense verbs, count and noncount nouns, and appositives are mostly correct. There are a few grammar problems, but ideas come across clearly. ■ **Spelling and Mechanics:** Paragraph has some spelling and/or punctuation mistakes.

1 **Developing**	■ **Content:** Paragraph does not present much information about a holiday and its foods or contains too many unrelated ideas. ■ **Organization:** Paragraph does not include a topic sentence. Order of ideas is confusing. Appositives and *such as* are not used or are used incorrectly throughout. ■ **Vocabulary:** Words are limited or repeated, and/or there are too many mistakes to understand the ideas. ■ **Grammar:** Paragraph contains present tense verb mistakes, and count and noncount noun mistakes. There are many grammar problems, making the ideas difficult to follow. ■ **Spelling and Mechanics:** Many distracting spelling and/or punctuation mistakes.

 7 **Peer Sharing** Show your paper to another student. Does he or she understand your paragraph? Does he or she think you need to add any other information?

8 **Writing the Second Draft** Rewrite your paragraph using your rubric evaluation. Then give your paragraph to your teacher for comments and corrections. When your teacher returns your paper, ask him or her about any comments or corrections you don't understand.

9 **Summarizing Your Strengths and Challenges** When your teacher returns your paragraph, look at the comments. If you don't understand something, ask about it. Then make a list of things you do well and things you need to work on.

What Do You Think?

Yin and Yang Foods
Some Chinese believe that there are yang and yin foods. Yang foods give you energy, and yin foods calm you. Yang foods are often spicy and warming, and yin foods are bland and cooling. Examples of yang foods are: chilies, chocolate, and coffee. Some examples of yin foods are: almonds, honey, and grapes.

Classifying Foods
Do you think that foods can influence the way that you feel? Are there ways to categorize foods based on how they make you feel? Write about these topics for 10 minutes in your journal. Then share your ideas with a partner.

1 **Sharing Your Writing and Pictures** Find pictures of the holiday celebration you described in your paragraph. Bring family pictures or pictures from magazines or the Internet to class. In small groups, read your paragraphs aloud and show each other the pictures.

2 **Writing About Special Occasions** Find a classmate who is not from the same city or region as you. Choose a special occasion both of you celebrate—weddings or birthdays, for example. Individually, write about how you each celebrate the occasion. Then discuss the similarities and differences.

3 **Writing in Your Journal** Write in your journal for 10 minutes about one or more of the following topics.

1. Why I love (or dislike) holidays (or a particular holiday).

2. My favorite food.

3. My favorite restaurant or café.

4 **Writing a Recipe** Look at the recipe for tabouleh. Then write a recipe for one of your favorite holiday dishes. Collect all the students' recipes. Copy them, and make a recipe booklet for each student.

Tabouleh

- 1/2 cup bulgur (cracked wheat)
- 1 1/4 cups chopped parsley
- 1/3 cup chopped mint leaves
- 1 small onion
- 1 large tomato
- 1/4 cup lemon juice
- 4 Tbs. extra virgin olive oil
- salt to taste

Soak the bulgur in water for about 2 hours, then rinse and drain water. Chop the parsley, mint, and green onions very fine. Dice the tomato. Combine all ingredients including the bulgur. Add salt to taste, lemon juice, olive oil, and mix well. Serve in a bowl with crackers or pita bread.

▲ *Add water to the bulgur.*

▲ *Squeeze out the water.*

▲ *Chop the parsley.*

▲ *Mix the ingredients together.*

5 **Researching a Holiday** Do an Internet search about a holiday in another country. Use a search engine like Google™ to find out about the holiday's special foods. Tell the class about the holiday and the foods associated with it.

Self-Assessment Log

In this chapter, you worked through the activities listed below. How much did they help you to become a better writer? Check *A lot*, *A little*, or *Not at all*.

	A lot	A little	Not at all
I practiced ordering information from general to specific.	❏	❏	❏
I created a graphic organizer that showed different levels of detail.	❏	❏	❏
I used count and noncount nouns.	❏	❏	❏
I gave examples with *such as*.	❏	❏	❏
I used appositives.	❏	❏	❏
I learned how to punctuate lists and appositives.	❏	❏	❏
I practiced forming plural nouns.	❏	❏	❏
I used a writing rubric to evaluate my first draft.	❏	❏	❏
(Add something) _____	❏	❏	❏

4

In the Community

> **❝**We must learn to live together as brothers or perish together as fools.**❞**

—Martin Luther King, Jr.
American civil rights movement leader, clergyman, and
Nobel Peace Prize winner (1929–1968)

Connecting to the Topic

1 Is this community similar to where you live? Why or why not?

2 Would you like to live in a place like this? Why or why not?

3 Have you ever visited a place like this? Explain.

Exploring Ideas

▲ Many communities offer a wide variety of activities.

1 **Describing Places to See and Things to Do** Look at the photos above. In small groups, discuss the following questions:

1. What are the people in the pictures doing?

2. In your own community, which of these activities do you participate in?

3. Which of these activities do you like or dislike? Why?

2 **Free Writing** Write for 5 minutes about your city or town. What do you like about it? What is there to do and see? When you write, don't worry about grammar or form. Just write as much as you can.

▶ Even small towns have community activities.

Building Vocabulary

3 **Brainstorming Vocabulary** In this chapter, you will write an informal letter to a friend, inviting him or her to stay with you. Fill in the blanks below with places your friend can visit or things she or he can do with you. List as many places and things as you can.

Places to Visit

1. _museum_   4. _____

2. _____   5. _____

3. _____   6. _____

Things to Do

Inside   **Outside**

1. _eat at a restaurant_   4. _____

2. _____   5. _____

3. _____   6. _____

4 **Comparing Vocabulary Lists** Compare your list with other students' lists. Do you want to add or change anything?

 5 **Generating New Vocabulary through Discussion** Many activities include the verb *go*. Some examples are *go sightseeing*, *go swimming*, *go fishing*, *go camping*, *go on a picnic*, or *go to the movies*. Work with a partner. Try to think of five more activities with *go*. Then share your list with the class.

6 **Creating a Map** In your letter, you will give your friend directions to your home from the nearest highway or major landmark. Work in groups to draw a map that shows the route to each student's home. Think about these questions:

1. Will your friend have to travel on a highway?

2. If so, how will she or he get from the highway to your home?

3. Are there any important landmarks (such as a lake, tall building, park, etc.) to help her or him find your house?

Organizing Ideas

ORGANIZING PARAGRAPHS IN A LETTER

Your letter will have three paragraphs. Each paragraph will have a different purpose.

1. The first paragraph will say *hello,* discuss the visit, and describe some of the activities you and your friend can do.
2. The second paragraph will give directions to your home.
3. The last paragraph will have only one or two sentences.
   The purpose of this paragraph is to say *good-bye* and end the letter.

---

7 **Ordering Ideas in a Letter** Look at the following sentences. Decide which paragraph of a letter they belong in. Write 1, 2, or 3 on the line before each sentence.

a. __1__ We can also go to a baseball game.

b. _____ There's a gas station on the corner.

c. _____ There's a concert at the City Auditorium.

d. _____ Make a left turn on Maple Avenue.

e. _____ It won't be hard to find my house.

f. _____ It won't be easy to get theater tickets.

g. _____ I'm glad to hear that you are doing well.

h. _____ See you in two weeks.

Using Graphic Organizers

Strategy

Giving Directions
When we give directions, we list step-by-step instructions for someone to follow.
You can use a graphic organizer to help you give the instructions clearly.

8 **Analyzing a Graphic Organizer** Look at the graphic organizer below. On the left are the directions. On the right is other information. Cross out information that is not necessary.

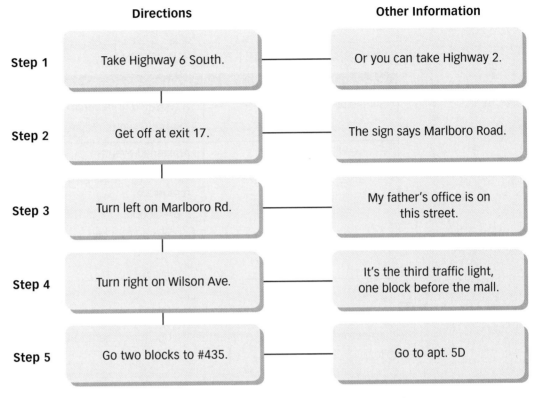

	Directions	**Other Information**
Step 1	Take Highway 6 South.	Or you can take Highway 2.
Step 2	Get off at exit 17.	The sign says Marlboro Road.
Step 3	Turn left on Marlboro Rd.	My father's office is on this street.
Step 4	Turn right on Wilson Ave.	It's the third traffic light, one block before the mall.
Step 5	Go two blocks to #435.	Go to apt. 5D

▲ A graphic organizer for giving directions

 9 **Creating a Graphic Organizer** Use the map you created in Activity 6 on page 61, and create a graphic organizer for the directions to your home. Give your map and the graphic organizer to a classmate. Can he or she understand your directions? Is there enough or too much information?

▲ Maps are useful for travelers.

Part 2 | Developing Writing Skills

Developing Cohesion and Clarity

CHOOSING THE CORRECT VERB TENSE

Forms	Notes and Examples
Simple present	A repeated or habitual action in the present: **Example** I <u>go</u> to the movies every Friday.
Future with *be going to*	A planned event: **Example** We'<u>re going to</u> go to the beach tomorrow. A prediction: **Example** She'<u>s going to</u> pass the test.

1 **Adding the Correct Verb to Sentences** Complete the paragraph below with the correct forms of the verbs in parentheses. Use the present tense or the future with *be going to*.

There ___are___ (be) many things to do here. I'm sure that we _____
1   2
(have) a good time. It _____ (be) hot, so bring your bathing suit.
3

There _____ (be) a beach very near my home.
4

I _____ (know) you like music, and the London
5

Symphony _____ (give) a concert on Saturday
6

afternoon. That night my sister _____ (have) a
7

birthday party. She's _____ (be) sixteen! On Sun-
8

days, we usually _____ (go) to a park for a picnic.
9

▲ A birthday cake

USING PREPOSITIONS

Prepositions often show:

Place	Direction
Examples	**Examples**
The shoe store is <u>in</u> the mall.	Take Highway 6 <u>to</u> Exit 14.
The concert is <u>at</u> the music hall.	Turn right <u>onto</u> Apple Avenue.
The school is <u>behind</u> the post office.	Drive <u>down</u> Main Street.
	Distance
There's a store <u>on</u> { the right. the left. the corner. Main Street.	**Example**
	Go straight <u>for</u> two blocks.

2 **Identifying Prepositions** Circle the prepositions of place, direction, and distance in the following paragraph. Then exchange papers with another student and compare your answers.

Take Route 44 south (to) Exit 12. Turn right at the first light. You will be on Maple Avenue. Go straight down Maple Avenue for two miles. At the corner of Bryant and Maple, you will see an elementary school. Turn right at the first street after the school. The name of the street is Roosevelt Drive. Go straight for five blocks. Then make a left turn onto Broadmoor. My apartment building isn't difficult to find. It's on the left, Number 122. You can park your car behind the building.

3 **Adding Prepositions to Sentences** Complete the paragraph below with the prepositions in the box. There may be more than one possible answer, and you can use the prepositions more than once.

at	for	on	to

I live in the old part of the city. Take the number 5 bus. Get off ___at___ Franklin Street. You will see a large church down the street.
₁

Walk _____ the church and turn right. Walk two blocks and turn
₂

left _____ Smith's Drugstore. You will be _____ Ames Avenue. Go
₃ ₄

straight on Ames _____ two blocks. Then turn left _____ the cor-
₅ ₆

ner of Ames and Findlay. My house is the third one _____ the left.
₇

4 Using Prepositions to Give Directions Use the map below to give directions to a partner.

Student A

Give directions from:

the post office to the library.

the elementary school to the hospital.

Student B

Give directions from:

the supermarket to the park.

the supermarket to the library.

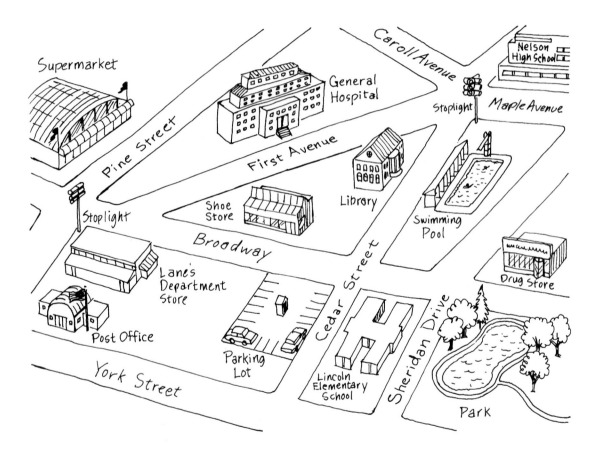

▲ A map can help you give directions.

USING *THERE*

There is sometimes used with *be* to introduce a subject and to say that something exists in a certain location.

Examples

<u>There</u> <u>is</u> a hotel near my house.

<u>There</u> <u>aren't</u> many places to park on my street.

There can also refer to a specific place.

Examples

I like New York. I go <u>there</u> every year.

You'll see a big church on the corner. Turn right <u>there</u>.

There can be used both ways in the same sentence.

Examples

I like New York City. <u>There's</u> a beautiful park <u>there</u>.

USING *IT* AND *THEY*

It can be used to describe the weather or a situation.

Examples

<u>It</u> is rainy today.

<u>It</u> isn't difficult to find my house.

<u>It</u> is crowded in the city on Saturdays.

It and *they* can also be used as pronouns.

Examples

I live in Chicago. <u>It</u> is a very busy but interesting place.

I like the people I've met in Morocco. <u>They</u> are very nice.

5 **Analyzing the Use of *There* and *It*** Look at the sentences below. Circle *there* and *it* when they refer to a specific place or thing. Underline *there* when it introduces a place. Underline *it* when it describes a situation or the weather.

1. <u>There</u> is a supermarket on the corner. (It) has a big red and white sign.

2. The museum is very interesting. I like to go there.

3. We can't have a picnic. It's rainy today.

4. I like New York City. There is a beautiful park there.

5. It is difficult to find housing in New York City.

6 **Completing Sentences with *There* and *It*.** Complete the following paragraph with *there* and *it*.

    <u>*There*</u> are many things to see in Washington DC. _____ is a
      1   2

very interesting city. I spend a few weeks _____ every year. In the
                                        3

center of the city, _____ is a large open area. People call _____
                        4   5

the mall. _____ are many museums _____. _____ is also a very
        6   7   8

large, famous structure. _____ is called the Washington Monument.
                          9

---

7 **Writing the First Draft** Write a draft of your letter. In the first paragraph, describe what you and your friend are going to do during the visit. In the second paragraph, give directions to your home. In the third paragraph, say *good-bye* and tell your friend how excited you are about the visit.

Part 3   Revising and Editing

Revising for Content and Editing for Form

1 **Revising for Content** Review the following letter for content. Mark where you would divide the letter into three paragraphs. Don't worry about misspelled words and other errors for now.

                                              June 15, 20___

Dear Moustapha, I'm very glad that you visit me next week. We will to have a good time. It's easy to find my house. Make left turn at the corner of Broadway and Fifth Street. Drive down Fifth two blocks. Make a right turn on Henry Street. There are a park on the corner. My house is on the left side. It are number 150. the weather is warm so we can going hiking and swimming. Please to bring your photo album. I want see the pictures of your family.

Salutation   **Date**

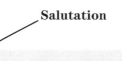

July 12, 20__

Dear Bill,

    I'm writing to say, "Hello" and to tell you about your upcoming visit. There's a lot to do here, and I'm sure we'll have a great time. On Saturday afternoon, we can go to a basketball game. I think I can get tickets. In the evening, we're going to go to Randy's house for dinner. After dinner we can go to a rock concert. I'm going to try to get tickets. If you want, on Sunday we can play tennis in the morning. There are tennis courts right near my house. In the afternoon, we can visit the planetarium. It's a very interesting place.

    It's easy to find my house. Just take Highway 47 east to Exit 5. Turn left at the first light. Then you will be on Bradford Boulevard. Go straight on Bradford for three miles. Then turn left on Apple. You will see a large supermarket on your left. Go to the second light. Make a right turn on Woodgate Road. My building is on the right, three houses from the corner. It's number 417.

Body

    I'm excited for your visit. See you in two weeks.

Closing

    Sincerely,

    Steve

Date The date usually appears in the upper right-hand corner of a letter. The order of the date is month, day, year. Capitalize the name of the month, and put a comma after the day and before the year. Do not use a comma in the year.

    Example April 4, 2007

Salutation Most letters begin with *Dear.* Use the name that you usually call the person. In an informal letter, a comma goes after the name.

    Examples   Dear Professor Ibrahimi,   Dear Mr. and Mrs. White,

                Dear Dr. Fitzgerald,   Dear Sen Lu,

Body Indent each paragraph. In letters, paragraphs may have only one or two sentences. Although it is important to write each paragraph about a different topic, the paragraphs in a letter do not always begin with a topic sentence.

Closing The closing of a letter begins either at the left or in the center of the page. There are many different closings. The closing that you choose depends on your relationship with the person you are writing to.

    Examples Regards,   Best wishes,   Fondly,   Love,

                for informal letters   for letters to close friends or relatives

2 **Editing for Form** Rewrite the letter in Activity 1 on page 68 on the lines below. Use correct letter form, and make any other corrections you feel are necessary.

_____

_____

_____

_____

_____

_____

_____

_____

_____

_____

_____

ADDRESSING AN ENVELOPE

The following illustrates the correct way to address an envelope:

Carol Martin
128 Lake Drive, Apt. 8
Muskegon, Michigan 49441 U.S.A.

Return Address

Stamp

Address

Mr. and Mrs. Daniel Kaufman
432 St. George Street
Toronto, Ontario
CANADA M56 2V8

Return Address Write your address in the top left-hand corner of the envelope.

Address Write the address clearly. You may want to print it. Make sure the address is complete. If there is an apartment number, be sure to include it. It is also important to use the zip code or the postal code.

3 **Addressing an Envelope** Correct the following address and write it on the envelope below. Write your name and address as the return address.

Mary pirewali, 256 rose avenue, san jose 95101 calif united states.

Evaluating Your Writing

4 **Using a Rubric** Read the rubric below with your class. Then use the rubric to score your paragraph.

Score	Description
3 **Excellent**	■ **Content:** Letter includes salutation, clear directions, information about places to see and/or things to do, and a closing. ■ **Organization:** Letter has three paragraphs; each paragraph serves a clear purpose. ■ **Vocabulary:** Vocabulary is clear, varied, and used correctly throughout. ■ **Grammar:** Subjects and verbs agree, and *be going to*, prepositions, and pronouns are used correctly. There are very few grammar problems, and the meaning is clear. ■ **Spelling and Mechanics:** Most words are spelled correctly, and punctuation is correct. Correct letter form is used.

2 **Adequate**	■ **Content:** Letter presents some information about what to see and do; directions may be unclear. ■ **Organization:** Letter has three paragraphs, but focus of all three may not be clear. ■ **Vocabulary:** Vocabulary is clear and varied, but some words may not be used correctly. ■ **Grammar:** Subjects and verbs mostly agree, *be going to* is used correctly, prepositions and pronouns are mostly used correctly. ■ **Spelling and Mechanics:** Most words are spelled correctly, and punctuation is correct. Correct letter form is used.
1 **Developing**	■ **Content:** Letter does not present much information about what to see, and there are many unrelated details. Directions and/or closing are not included. ■ **Organization:** Letter does not have three paragraphs. Purpose of paragraphs is not clear. ■ **Vocabulary:** Vocabulary is limited and/or repetitive. Many errors make ideas hard to understand. ■ **Grammar:** Prepositions, pronouns, and *be going to*, are not used or are used incorrectly. Subject-verb errors and several other grammatical errors make the letter difficult to understand. ■ **Spelling and Mechanics:** Many distracting spelling and/or punctuation mistakes. Correct letter form is not used.

 5 Peer Sharing Exchange letters with another student. Discuss the letters. Is your partner interested in knowing more about what there is to do in your town? What can you tell him or her?

6 Writing the Second Draft Rewrite your letter using your rubric evaluation. Then give your letter to your teacher for comments and corrections. When your teacher returns your paper, ask him or her about any comments or corrections you don't understand.

7 Evaluating Your Progress Write a journal entry about your writing. Do you feel that it is improving? If so, how? What areas still need work?

What Do You Think?

Evaluating Your Community's Services

With your class, research and discuss the types of activities that are available at your school and in your community (sports, music, clubs, and so on). Answer the following questions:

1. Is there a variety of activities?
2. Are there enough activities available for people of all ages?
3. Are there many free or inexpensive activities?
4. What kinds of activities do you or your family do?
5. Are there any that are not available that you would like to have?

Part 4 Expansion Activities

1 Getting Directions Exchange letters with another student. Try to draw a map from the highway to your partner's home. Then pretend you are the friend, and write a reply. Ask any questions you may have about the visit or the directions.

2 Inviting a Classmate to Your House Pretend you want to invite a friend from your class to your home. Write your classmate an informal letter inviting him or her. Explain how to get from school to your home. Draw a small map.

3 Writing in Your Journal Write for 10 or 15 minutes about one or both of the following topics:

1. Compare the place you are living now with a place you lived in the past. Describe the places. Which one do you like best? Why?
2. Write about your community's transportation. How do people generally get around? Is the transportation good or bad?

4 **Researching a City or Town** Do an Internet search for your city/town or a city/town that you would like to visit. Use Google™ or another search engine to find out about the topics below. Share your information with the class.

1. community events
2. parks
3. museums
4. sporting events
5. other tourist sites

▲ Hagia Sofia, Istanbul Turkey.

Self-Assessment Log

In this chapter, you worked through the activities listed below. How much did they help you to become a better writer? Check *A lot*, *A little*, or *Not at all*.

	A lot	A little	Not at all
I described places to see and things to do in my community.	❏	❏	❏
I learned to organize paragraphs in a letter.	❏	❏	❏
I used a graphic organizer to write directions.	❏	❏	❏
I practiced using the present tense.	❏	❏	❏
I used *be going to* to write about future plans.	❏	❏	❏
I practiced using prepositions of location, direction, and distance.	❏	❏	❏
I learned to address an envelope.	❏	❏	❏
I used a writing rubric to evaluate my first draft.	❏	❏	❏
(Add something) _____	❏	❏	❏

_____

5

Home

❝ My home is not a place, it is people. **❞**

—Lois McMaster Bujold
American writer (1949–)

Connecting to the Topic

1 What kind of home is this?

2 Would you like to live in a home like this? Why or why not?

3 What kinds of homes have you lived in?

Exploring Ideas

Strategy

In this chapter, you will write a paragraph about an important time in your life. You can use a lifeline to organize events from your life in chronological order; that is, the order in which they happened.

1 **Creating a Lifeline** Create a lifeline, a kind of time line. Follow the steps below.

1. Draw a line down the middle of a piece of paper. At the top of the line, write "0", and at the bottom, write your current age.

2. To the left of the line, list important events in the order that they happened.

3. To the right of the line, write your feelings about the events. You don't need to use complete sentences.

4. Draw pictures and symbols to illustrate your lifeline.

Building Vocabulary

 2 **Generating Vocabulary through Discussion** Join a group of three students and discuss your lifelines. Ask each other questions. Notice what the other students think is interesting about your life. Make a list of any new words that you hear, and look up any words that you don't understand.

Organizing Ideas

Strategy

Limiting Information
You can't write about your whole life in one paragraph, so you'll need to limit the information you'll include. One way to do this is to decide which period in your life would be the most interesting to read about. Things that make a period of life interesting to read about are: an important or unusual event that occurred, a challenge that you overcame, or a dream that you realized. The better you define the period of time you're going to write about, the easier it will be to write a focused, cohesive paragraph about it.

3 Choosing the Best Topic Join a group of three students, and look at the lifeline below. Discuss which part of the person's life would make a good topic for a paragraph and why.

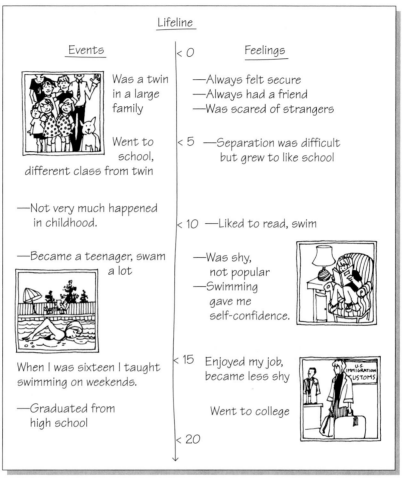

▲ A lifeline

4 Defining Your Topic Look at your lifeline and choose a part of your life to write about. As you decide, consider the following questions:

1. Which part of my life is more interesting than others? Why?

2. Which part of my life is important to me? Why?

3. Does the period of my life I've chosen center around one event or theme?

5 **Discussing Your Topic** Show a partner your lifeline, and tell him or her which period of your life you've chosen to write about. Discuss your reasons.

6 **Brainstorming Ideas** On a separate piece of paper, list as many ideas as you can about the period of time in your life that you plan to write about. Then review your ideas, and circle the most important ones.

Writing Topic Sentences

7 **Choosing the Best Topic Sentence** Look at the ideas and topic sentences listed for the two paragraphs outlined below. For each paragraph, circle the number of the topic sentence that you think gives the main idea. Discuss your choices with your classmates.

▲ Twins

Paragraph 1

- Was born a twin—very important to childhood

- Always had a friend, felt secure

- Was in different classes than sister

- Separation from sister at school was difficult

- Didn't do well at school at first

Topic Sentences

1. Being a twin was both a benefit and a challenge.

2. Because I had a twin sister, I felt secure.

3. I didn't like school because I was in different classes from my twin sister.

Paragraph 2

- Teenage years difficult

- Liked to read, was shy, not popular

- Was a good swimmer

- Taught swimming on weekends

- This gave me self-confidence and I was happy and secure by 19.

Topic Sentences

1. I wasn't popular as a teenager.

2. As a teenager, I taught swimming on weekends.

3. My teenage years were very difficult at first, but they ended happily.

8 **Writing a Draft Topic Sentence** Look at the notes you wrote in Activity 6. Write two possible topic sentences for your paragraph. Show your notes and topic sentences to another student. Which one does he or she think is better? Why? Which one do you think is better? Why?

Strategy

Writing a Title

The title for your paragraph should capture its main idea, and it should also make someone *want* to read your paragraph. When you write a title, try to hint at or evoke an interesting aspect of the content of your paragraph.

The title goes in the middle of the top line of the paper and is not a complete sentence.

In the title, capitalize the first word and all of the important words. Don't capitalize the following kinds of words (unless they're the first word in the title):

- **conjunctions**: *and*, *but*, or, *so*
- **articles**: *a*, *an*, and *the*
- **prepositions**: *at*, *by*, *for*, *in*, *of*, *on*, *out*, *to*, *up*, *about*, and *with*

9 **Correcting Titles** Rewrite the titles below with the correct capitalization.

1. an exciting life _____

2. all's well that ends well _____

3. a gift of hope _____

4. the best years of my life _____

5. going away _____

6. a happy ending _____

7. life in a new city _____

8. best friends _____

9. a new beginning _____

10. a wonderful experience _____

10 **Choosing the Best Titles** The titles below go with the paragraphs outlined on page 80. Put a checkmark by the titles that you like. Why do you like them? Discuss your choices with the class.

Paragraph 1	Paragraph 2
My Childhood	Growing Up
Born a Twin	Unhappy Teens
Difficult School Years	Teenage Years
My Childhood as a Twin	Teaching Swimming

11 **Writing Draft Titles** Look at your paragraph notes and write two possible titles for your paragraph. Show your notes and titles to another student. Which one does he or she think is better? Why? Which one do you think is better? Why?

Part 2 Developing Writing Skills

Developing Cohesion and Clarity

1 **Using the Past Tense** Complete the following paragraph with the correct past tense forms of the verbs in parentheses. For the spelling of verbs with -ed, see Appendix 1.

Because I _____ (be) born a twin, I
_____ (have) a very different childhood from most
people. There _____ (be) always someone to play with,
and I always _____ (have) a friend. My mother said that,
when we were young, my sister and I _____ (feed) each
other, _____ (play) together, and _____ (cry)
when strangers came near. We _____ (do) everything together. When my sister _____ (need) special shoes, I
_____ (want) them too. But life as a twin _____
(not be) always great. My mother _____ (be) always
tired because she _____ (work) so hard, and my father

_____ (complain) that the house was too noisy with two
₁₄
screaming babies. Although I don't mind being a twin, I wouldn't want to
have them.

2 **Writing Sentences with Past Tense Verbs** Look at your paragraph notes,
and write four or five sentences with past tense verbs. Use past tense verbs only for
completed events. Share your sentences with a group of three students.

COMBINING SENTENCES WITH TIME WORDS AND *BECAUSE*
When you write a paragraph that describes a sequence of events, you can use time
words to combine sentences. Some common time words are *before*, *after*, *when*, and
as soon as.

Examples
<u>Before</u> I started school, I was very happy.
<u>After</u> I left high school, I got a job.
<u>When</u> my family said good-bye, I was very sad.
<u>As soon as</u> I came to the United States, I got sick.

You can also combine sentences with *because* to show cause and effect.

Example
<u>Because</u> she worked hard, my mother was always tired.

---

3 **Completing Sentences with Time Words, Conjunctions, and**
Because Complete the sentences in the paragraph with *before*, *after*, *when*, *because*,
and, *but*, or *so.* More than one answer may be possible.

I had a typical childhood____*before*____
₁
my life changed._____ I was four-
₂
teen, we moved from our small village to Kara-
chi, a big city in Pakistan. _____ we
₃
moved, life in the country was wonderful for me,
but _____ I started school in Kara-
₄
chi, I became shy and nervous. Some of the other
girls in my classes were mean, _____
₅

▲ Maryam is from Pakistan.

they laughed at my country ways. _____ I didn't fit in, I became more interested in books. I always liked biology, _____
7
I started to read about medicine. I was very unhappy at the time, _____ I didn't have many friends. _____ I got to
8   9
the university, my life was much better.

4 Completing Sentences with Information from Your Life Finish the sentences below using information about your life.

1. When I became a teenager, *I had a strong desire to travel.* _____

_____

2. I decided to study English because _____

_____

3. When I was a child, I _____

_____

4. After I left high school, I _____

_____

5. Before I started this class, _____

_____

PUNCTUATING SENTENCES WITH DEPENDENT CLAUSES

When you add a time word or *because* to the beginning of a sentence, it becomes a dependent clause. A dependent clause cannot stand alone. It is a sentence fragment.

Examples

<u>When</u> I was five.
<u>Because</u> my father had a new job. } sentence fragments

You must combine a dependent clause with an independent clause. An independent clause can stand alone.

Example

We moved to Caracas.

If the dependent clause appears at the beginning of a sentence, use a comma after it.

Example
When I was five, we moved to Caracas.
Because my father had a new job, we moved to Caracas.

If the dependent clause appears at the end of the sentence, don't add a comma.

Examples
We moved to Caracas when I was five.
We moved to Caracas because my father had a new job.

---

5 **Combining Sentences** Combine the sentences below with the words in parentheses. Use a comma if necessary. You might have to change the order of the sentences.

1. I was a good student. I got a scholarship. (because) *Because I was a good student, I got a scholarship.*

2. I graduated from high school. I was 16. (when) _____

3. My father died. My mother went to work. (after) _____

4. I found a job. I finished high school. (as soon as) _____

5. I stopped studying. I was unhappy. (so) _____

6 **Writing Sentences with Time Words and *Because*** Look at your paragraph notes, and use each of the words below to write one sentence about the time of your life you plan to write your paragraph about.

1. before *Before I started school, I taught myself to read.* _____

2. because _____

3. after _____

4. when _____

5. as soon as _____

7 **Writing the First Draft** Write your paragraph about an important time in your life. Don't forget to do the following:

- Use the topic sentence and the notes you wrote earlier in the chapter.
- Combine some sentences with conjunctions, time words, and *because*.
- Use the past tense when you write about completed actions.
- Include a title.

Part 3 | Revising and Editing

Revising for Content and Editing for Form

1 **Revising for Content** Review the paragraph below for content. Combine sentences with *and*, *but*, and *so*. Don't worry about misspelled words and other errors for now.

How i became a jazz musician

I fall in love with jazz when I am five years old. I always heared jazz in the streets but for my fifth birthday my brother tooks me to a concert. There I saw a great saxophonist I decided to learn to play the saxophone. First I need a saxophone, I ask my father. My father say he no have money for a saxophone. I work for my brother, uncles, and cousins. I made a little money then my father see I work hard. He gave me money for a saxophone. I listen to recordings. My brother teach me. I practice every day. Soon I am a good saxophone player.

2 **Editing Practice: Independent and Dependent Clauses** For each of the sentences below, write *correct* if the punctuation is correct, or rewrite the sentence with correct punctuation if it is wrong.

1. Before we moved here we used to have many friends and relatives nearby.
Before we moved here, we used to have many friends and relatives nearby.

2. Because my uncle was an engineer, he sent me to engineering school.

_____

_____

3. I left the farm as soon as I could.

_____

_____

4. We moved to Colorado. Because the doctors said I needed a dry climate.

_____

_____

5. When I first came here I loved the excitement of New York.

_____

_____

6. I came to the city, when I was five.

_____

_____

3 **Editing for Form** Edit the paragraph on page 86 for form. Correct past tense verb forms, and make other changes you think are necessary.

Evaluating Your Writing

4 **Using a Rubric** Read the rubric below with your class. Then use the rubric to score your paragraph.

Score	Description
3 **Excellent**	■ **Content:** Paragraph presents information about a specific period in the writer's life. ■ **Organization:** Paragraph is introduced by a topic sentence, and all sentences connect to this main idea. Information is organized in chronological order. ■ **Vocabulary:** Vocabulary is descriptive and used correctly throughout. ■ **Grammar:** Past tense is used correctly, and sentences are combined with time words and _because_. There are no sentence fragments. ■ **Spelling and Mechanics:** Most words are spelled correctly, and punctuation is correct.

2 Adequate	<ul><li>**Content:** Paragraph presents information about a period of the writer's life, but details may be limited.</li><li>**Organization:** Ideas are introduced by a topic sentence. Information may not be organized in chronological order.</li><li>**Vocabulary:** Most vocabulary is used correctly.</li><li>**Grammar:** Past tense is mostly used correctly. At least one sentence is combined with a time word or *because*.</li><li>**Spelling and Mechanics:** Paragraph includes some spelling and/or punctuation mistakes.</li></ul>
1 Developing	<ul><li>**Content:** Paragraph does not present much information about the writer's life, or there are too many (unrelated) details.</li><li>**Organization:** Paragraph ideas do not connect to the topic sentence, or there is no topic sentence.</li><li>**Vocabulary:** Vocabulary is limited, and/or there are too many mistakes to understand the ideas.</li><li>**Grammar:** Past tense is not used correctly. Many grammar problems make ideas difficult to understand.</li><li>**Spelling and Mechanics:** Paragraph includes many distracting spelling and/or punctuation mistakes.</li></ul>

 5 Peer Sharing Exchange paragraphs with another student. Tell your partner what you like best about his or her paragraph. Ask questions about anything that is unclear.

6 Writing the Second Draft Rewrite your paragraph using your rubric evaluation. Then give your paragraph to your teacher for comments and corrections. When your teacher returns your paper, ask him or her about any comments or corrections you don't understand.

WRITING WITH COMPUTERS

When you revise, you should keep the earlier drafts of your work. They can be useful for several reasons. You or your teacher might want to compare drafts. You also might decide to use words or phrases that you had erased. Save a new draft by giving it a different name—for example, **My Life_ draft 2**.

What Do You Think?

Birth Order

Many people believe that birth order influences the kind of people we become. For instance, some say that the first-borns are usually independent high-achievers and natural leaders. They also say that middle-borns are usually quiet people-pleasers who try to keep the peace at any cost. Finally, believers in birth order research say that last-borns are often rebellious and extroverted. They make people feel comfortable and like to take risks. Only-borns are comfortable with responsibility and very organized.

Thinking About Your Birth Order

Do you think your birth order has influenced the person you've become? Why? Why not? Write about this for 10 minutes in your journal.

Part 4   Expansion Activities

 1 Sharing Your Writing Bring in photographs of the time in your life you wrote about. Share your paragraphs with a group, and discuss the experiences you described. Did other students have similar experiences?

 2 Interviewing a Friend Interview a friend or relative about his or her life. Then choose one part of the person's life, and write about it.

3 Writing from the Imagination Invent a life for yourself. Write about the life you wish you'd had. Use the past tense.

Example

I was born into a very wealthy family. We lived in Venice for eight years. Then we moved to Florence . . .

4 Writing in Your Journal Write in your journal for 10 minutes about one of the following topics:

1. The happiest time in my life

2. The saddest time in my life

5 **Researching a Famous Person in History** Use a search engine to find information on the life of a famous person. Choose someone who is no longer living. Answer the questions below. Create a time line for the person. Then write a paragraph about an important event or time in his or her life.

1. When did this person live?

2. What was his or her childhood like?

3. Was he or she married? Did he or she have children?

4. Why was he or she famous?

5. When and where did he or she die?

▲ Albert Einstein, physicist

Self-Assessment Log

In this chapter, you worked through the activities listed below. How much did they help you to become a better writer? Check *A lot*, *A little*, or *Not at all*.

	A lot	A little	Not at all
I used a time line to organize information in chronological order.	❏	❏	❏
I learned to write a topic sentence for a narrative paragraph.	❏	❏	❏
I learned to limit information in a narrative paragraph.	❏	❏	❏
I learned to punctuate titles.	❏	❏	❏
I used the past tense to talk about my life.	❏	❏	❏
I combined sentences with time words and *because*.	❏	❏	❏
I learned to punctuate sentences with dependent clauses.	❏	❏	❏
I used a writing rubric to evaluate my first draft.	❏	❏	❏
(Add something) _____	❏	❏	❏

Cultures of the World

❝ A good writer is basically a story-teller, not a scholar or a redeemer of mankind. **❞**

—Isaac Bashevis Singer
Polish–born American writer (1904–1991)

Connecting to the Topic

1 What purpose do folktales serve?

2 Name some famous folktales from your country.

3 Describe your favorite folktale.

Exploring Ideas

Folktales

Every culture has its own folktales. These stories tell us a lot about the culture in earlier times. They tell us what values were held and how society was organized. Folktales are not written by one person or one at a time. Each story develops over many years. In this way, folktales come from the imagination of the whole culture.

Folktales are usually told in time sequence, and they do not usually include a lot of description. Because the stories were told aloud, they were kept simple so the storyteller and the listener could remember them.

1 Reading a Folktale Read the passage below. It is the beginning of a folktale from Saxony, a part of Germany.

▲ The king was tired, cold, and hungry.

One day, a good and powerful king, who was loved by all of the people in his kingdom, went for a ride alone in the forest. After hours of riding in an unfamiliar part of the forest, he got lost. He was tired, cold, and hungry. Just before nightfall, he found the hut of a poor miner. The miner was working, and his wife was home alone. She was cooking potatoes on the fire when she heard someone at the door.

The king asked her for help. "We are very poor," explained the miner's wife, "but we can give you potatoes for dinner and a blanket on the floor for a bed." The king gratefully accepted the kind woman's offer. He sat down to dinner with her and ate a large plate of potatoes. "These are better than the best beef," he exclaimed. Then he stretched out on the floor and quickly fell asleep.

Early the next morning, the king washed in the river and then returned to the hut. He thanked the woman for her kindness and gave her a gold coin. Then he left.

As soon as the miner returned home, his wife told him about the visitor. Then she showed her husband the gold coin. The husband realized that the visitor was the king, and he felt that the gold coin was too generous. He decided to take a bushel of potatoes to the king.

The miner went to the palace to see the king. "Your majesty," he said, "last night you gave my wife a gold coin for a hard bed and a plate of potatoes. You were too generous. Therefore, I have brought you a bushel of potatoes, which you said were better than the best beef. Please accept them."

The miner's words pleased the king. He wanted to reward him for his honesty, so he gave him a beautiful house and a small farm. The miner was very happy, and he returned to tell his wife the news.

The poor miner had a brother. His brother was rich but greedy, and jealous of anyone who had good luck. When he heard his brother's story, he was very upset.

Building Vocabulary

2 **Identifying Vocabulary Words** Find the words in the story that mean:

1. a small house   *hut* _____

2. a large container _____

3. selfish _____

4. a person who digs for coal _____

5. unselfish _____

6. a kind of meat _____

7. the home of a king _____

8. envious _____

3 **Using New Vocabulary** Join a group of three students. Take turns using each of the words above in a sentence that tells part of the story.

4 Generating New Vocabulary Through Discussion In small groups, look at the pictures below, and make up new endings to the story of the king and the miner. Choose one of the three endings to write about, or think of a different ending. Write down any new words you heard in your discussion, and look them up.

▲ The miner's brother steals his brother's gold coin.

▲ The miner's brother gives the king a horse.

▲ The miner's brother receives a bushel of corn from the king.

Organizing Ideas

5 Brainstorming Ideas for Your Story Ending On a separate piece of paper, write as many ideas as you can for the ending of your story. Use the questions below as a guide.

1. What did the brother decide to give the king?
2. Why did he decide to give the king a gift?
3. Was the king happy with the brother?
4. What did the king do?
5. How did the brother feel?

Using Graphic Organizers

Strategy

Using a Plot Diagram

In Chapter 5 you used a time line to organize events in chronological order. You can also use a plot diagram to order the events in a story.

A plot diagram has five parts: exposition, rising action, climax, falling action, and resolution. The **exposition** tells the background of the story, what happened before the rising action. The **rising action** shows the conflict in the story. It is an event that leads to the climax or turning point in the story. The **climax** is usually the most exciting or interesting part of the story. After the climax, is the **falling action**. During the falling action, all the conflicts start to be worked out. Finally, the story ends at the **resolution** where all the problems are solved.

The sequence of exposition, rising action, climax, falling action, and resolution can occur more than once in a story. Your story ending will include all five elements.

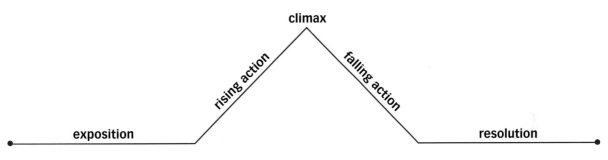

▲ A plot diagram

6 **Creating a Plot Diagram** Create a plot diagram for your story ending. If you get stuck, discuss your ideas with a partner. Use the graphic organizer below as a model.

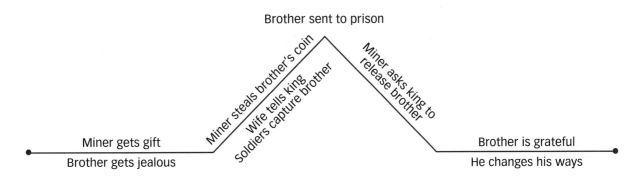

▲ A plot diagram for an ending to the story of the king and the miner

7 **Limiting Information** You will write your story ending in one paragraph, so it is important to limit what you say. Look at your graphic organizer. Does the sequence of events seem clear? Are there any details that are unnecessary to the story?

 8 **Sharing Your Ideas** Using your plot diagram, tell your story ending to another student, and discuss the following questions:

1. Is your story ending too complicated or difficult for the reader to understand?

2. Did you include too many events?

3. Will everything fit into one paragraph?

> ### Strategy
>
> **Writing a Title**
> The title of a story should be interesting and not too general. It should also hint at an interesting aspect of the story without telling the reader how the story will end.

9 **Choosing the Best Title** Which of the following do you think is a good title for the story you read? Circle the number. Why do you think it's good?

1. The Miner and the King

2. The Generous Brother and The Selfish Brother

3. A Gift for a Gift

4. The Magic Potatoes

Part 2 Developing Writing Skills

Developing Cohesion and Clarity

WRITING ABOUT TWO EVENTS THAT OCCURRED IN THE PAST

Use *when* and *while* to describe two events that occurred in the past.

To introduce an action that interrupted another action in the past, use *when.*

Example
The woman was cooking <u>when</u> the king knocked on the door.

You can also use *while* to introduce the longer action.

Example

<u>While</u> the woman was cooking, the king knocked on the door.

Note that the past continuous is used for the longer action, and the simple past is used for the interrupting action.

You can use *while* to describe two actions that were in progress at the same time.

Example

<u>While</u> the miner was working, his wife was helping the king.

Note that the past continuous is used for both actions.

Use *when* to describe an action that was followed by another action. The second action is often the result of the first action.

Example

<u>When</u> the miner's brother heard the story, he got jealous.

Note that the simple past is used for both actions.

---

1 **Combining Sentences with *When* and *While*** Combine the following sentences using *when* or *while*. More than one answer may be correct.

1. The king was hunting. He got lost in the forest.

The king was hunting when he got lost in the forest.

2. The king saw the hut. He decided to ask for help.

3. The miner was talking to the king. His wife was working at home.

4. The miner gave the potatoes to the king. The king was pleased.

5. The king gave the woman the coin. She was surprised.

2 **Writing Sentences with *When* and *While*** Look at the notes for your story ending and write three sentences: two with *when* and one with *while*.

Example

When the king saw the horse, he was very surprised.

_____

_____

_____

_____

_____

USING *AS SOON AS*

When you write about two events that occurred in the past, you can use *as soon as* to emphasize that one action happened immediately after another. The second action is often the result of the first action.

Examples

As soon as the miner got home, his wife told him the story.

As soon as she heard about the gift from the king, the miner's wife became very excited.

3 **Combining Sentences with *As Soon As*** Combine the following sentences with *as soon as*.

1. The brother heard the story. He decided to give the king a better gift.
   As soon as the brother heard the story, he decided to give the king
   a better gift.

2. The king talked to the brother. The king knew that he was a liar.

   _____

   _____

3. The king ate dinner. He fell asleep.

   _____

   _____

4. The miner got the farm. He quit his job.

   _____

   _____

4 **Writing Sentences with *As Soon As*** Look at the notes for your story-ending, and write two sentences with *as soon as.*

_____

USING *THEN*

When you write about a sequence of events in a story, you can use *then* to make the time sequence clear and not repeat the same words.

Compare:

I ran out of the house. After I ran out of the house, I saw a man in the street.

I ran out of the house. <u>Then</u> I saw a man in the street.

_____

5 **Rewriting Sentences Using *Then*** Rewrite the following sentences using *then.*

1. The king washed in the river. He thanked the woman and left.
The king washed in the river. Then he thanked the woman and left.

2. The woman gave the king a plate of potatoes. She gave him a blanket.
_____

3. The king gave the woman a coin. He gave the miner a house and a farm.
_____

4. The brother found a bushel of potatoes. He took them to the king.
_____

Strategy

Varying Time Words and Phrases
To make your writing interesting, it is important to vary the time words that you use to connect a sequence of events. You have learned the following time words: *when*, *while*, *before*, *after*, *then*, and *as soon as.*

---

 6 **Identifying Time Words** Look at the story of the miner and the king on pages 94 and 95. Make a list of the time words. Compare your list with another student's. Are there any words you missed?

after _____   _____

_____   _____

_____   _____

_____   _____

7 **Completing Sentences with Time Words** Complete the following sentences with one of the time words listed below. In some cases, more than one answer is correct, and the words can be used more than once.

> when   while   before   after   then   as soon as

1. _____When_____ the brother heard the story, he got jealous.

2. _____ the king met the miner's brother, he knew he was not sincere.

3. The miner and his wife were very happy _____ the king gave them the house.

4. The king left the miner's house _____ the miner returned home.

5. _____ the miner's brother got the king's gift, he was very angry.

6. The king gave the old woman some gold. _____ he left.

7. The miner was cleaning the house _____ his wife was cooking dinner.

8 **Writing the First Draft** Using the notes and sentences you wrote earlier in the chapter, write an ending to the folktale. Remember to use time words to connect ideas and show a sequence of events. Limit your paragraph to 150 to 170 words.

Part 3   Revising and Editing

Revising for Content and Editing for Form

1 **Revising for Content** Review the paragraph on page 103 for content. Make suggestions and comments on a separate piece of paper. Keep the following things in mind.

- Content: Is all the information necessary?
- Length: The paragraph should be 150 to 170 words.
- Sequence: Are time words used to show the sequence of events?

Don't worry about misspelled words and other errors for now.

When the miner's brother ridding home through the forest, he thought of a plan. He decided to give the king his best horse because he wanted the king to give him a gift like he gave his brother. So, as soon as he finished breakfast the next day, the brother went to the palace. The palace was not far from his house. It took the miner's brother a half hour to get there. When he got to the palace, he asked to see the king. The guard immediately took him to see the king. He gives the king his best horse.

▲ Outside the window, the king saw a beautiful horse.

The horse was magnificent. It was a big, black stallion. The miner's brother had a friend who sold stallions. The king knew that this was not an honest gift. He smiled and gave the brother a sack of potatoes. What could the greedy brother do? He lifted the heavy bushel and sadly left the room. As he was leaving, he heard the king laughing.

USING EDITING SYMBOLS

Your teacher might use some common editing symbols when reviewing your written work. In Chapter 1 you learned about the caret (^). Below are some other symbols and examples of how editing symbols are used.

sp wrong spelling

sp
He is a studint in Doha.   He is a student in Doha.

sf sentence fragment

sf
When I was ten. We moved to London.   When I was ten, we moved to London.

/ use lowercase (small letters)

The /Thief ran out the door.   The thief ran out the door.

Take out this word, letter, or punctuation.

Sylvia sang a song / while she washed the dishes.
Sylvia sang a song while she washed the dishes.

Add punctuation here.

The doctor arrived at ten o'clock○
The doctor arrived at ten o'clock.^

2 Editing for Form Edit the paragraph on page 103 for correct punctuation, grammar, and form. Use editing symbols.

Evaluating Your Writing

3 Using a Rubric Read the rubric below with your class. Then use the rubric to score your paragraph.

Score	Description
3 **Excellent**	■ **Content:** Paragraph concludes the folktale and contains all the relevant story elements. ■ **Organization:** Order of events is clear, time words are used, and no irrelevant information is included. ■ **Vocabulary:** Vocabulary is specific and used correctly throughout. ■ **Grammar:** Past tense verbs and time words are used correctly. ■ **Spelling and Mechanics:** Most words are spelled correctly, and there are few punctuation errors.
2 **Adequate**	■ **Content:** Paragraph concludes the folktale, but one or two story elements may be missing. ■ **Organization:** Events follow chronological order and time words are used, but paragraph may include some irrelevant information. ■ **Vocabulary:** Most vocabulary is used correctly. ■ **Grammar:** Past tense verbs and time words are mostly used correctly. ■ **Spelling and Mechanics:** Some spelling and/or punctuation mistakes.
1 **Developing**	■ **Content:** Paragraph does not conclude the folktale. Most or all story elements are missing. ■ **Organization:** Order of events is confusing, and/or ideas are confusing and unrelated to the story. ■ **Vocabulary:** Vocabulary is limited, and/or there are too many mistakes to understand the ideas. ■ **Grammar:** Paragraph includes several verb tense mistakes, making the story ending hard to understand. Time words are not used. ■ **Spelling and Mechanics:** Many distracting spelling and/or punctuation mistakes.

4 **Peer Sharing** Exchange paragraphs with another student. Compare your story endings. How are they different? How are they similar? Can you identify the exposition, rising action, climax, falling action, and resolution?

5 **Writing the Second Draft** Rewrite your paragraph using your rubric evaluation. Then give your paragraph to your teacher for comments and corrections. When your teacher returns your paper, ask him or her about any comments or corrections you don't understand.

What Do You Think?

Analyzing a Folktale Ending

Most folktales teach a lesson or moral. The real ending of the folktale in this chapter is the paragraph on page 103. Reread the paragraph and answer the following questions:

1. What can we learn about German culture from this folktale?

2. What is the moral of this story? Does the story teach this lesson well?

3. Are folktales with morals an effective way to pass down wisdom from generation to generation? Why? Why not?

4. How are morals and ideas passed down from generation to generation today?

TOEFL® IBT

Focus on Testing

Borrowing Key Words from Short Readings

The writing section of the TOEFL® Internet-Based Test (iBT)* includes one "integrated" task. For this you must use information from a short reading and a short listening passage to respond to a prompt (question). To strengthen the vocabulary in your response, you can borrow carefully from the reading and listening passages. Some hints for borrowing vocabulary:

- Borrow individual vocabulary items only. For example, it would be okay to borrow the words *accepted* or *sat down* from the story of the miner, but not an entire phrase like *reward him for his honesty.*

- Borrow vocabulary items that are hard to paraphrase, such as *miner, coin,* and *potato.*

- Borrow proper nouns (e.g., *Mr. Bradford, Saxony, World War II*).

Practice 1

Using the hints above for borrowing vocabulary, revise the folktale ending you wrote.

*TOEFL and TOEIC are registered trademarks of Educational Testing Service (ETS). This publication is not endorsed or approved by ETS.

Practice 2

Read the passage below. Then write three sentences on a separate piece of paper. Each one should state the main idea of each paragraph in the passage. Borrow vocabulary items from the reading as necessary.

Jung and Folktales

Carl Jung was a psychologist who studied folktales. Even though folktales are fiction, he said that they express a culture's important beliefs. He also said that humans share a "collective unconscious." This is a set of meaningful images common among people throughout the world. These images show up in folktales from widely different cultures.

For example, many folktales include a king (or other authority figure) who goes out into the countryside in disguise. There he is treated kindly by a poor farmer who doesn't know who his guest is. Eventually, the poor person is rewarded for his good deeds. This kind of tale expresses a belief that powerful forces see what we do even if we don't know it. People who are kind and respectful will be paid back for their generosity.

Folktales usually include at least one evil person or animal that threatens a person or a group. Usually, a good person or animal then fights the evil one and wins. Jung said that such tales express some very deep fears among humans. He believed that, by expressing these fears in a folktale, people can become less afraid of the world.

WRITING WITH COMPUTERS

Give your files names that you can remember. Be careful with abbreviations. **Go2p23** might make sense to you today, but if you have to look for the file next month, you won't be able to remember what it means.

Part 4   A Step Beyond

1 **Sharing Your Writing** Read your story ending to the other students in the class.

 2 **Writing the Beginning of a Story** Write the beginning of a folktale that you know. Give it to a classmate. She or he will write the ending

 3 **Rewriting a Folktale** Think of a folktale that you know. Rewrite it, changing the plot and giving it a new ending. Read the story to a group of students. Can they guess the original story?

4 **Writing in Your Journal** Write about a folktale that you learned as a child. What is the moral of the story? How has it affected your life?

 5 **Researching a Fable** Fables are stories with lessons that usually contain elements of fantasy. Aesop's fables are morality stories from Greece. On the Internet, find one of Aesop's fables. Write a plot diagram for the fable. Then tell the story to a partner.

Self-Assessment Log

In this chapter, you worked through the activities listed below. How much did they help you to become a better writer? Check *A lot*, *A little*, or *Not at all*.

	A lot	A little	Not at all
I read and discussed a folktale.	❏	❏	❏
I learned about story elements.	❏	❏	❏
I used a plot diagram.	❏	❏	❏
I used time words to describe a sequence of events.	❏	❏	❏
I practiced limiting information in a narrative paragraph.	❏	❏	❏
I used time words to write about events in the past.	❏	❏	❏
I learned to use editing symbols.	❏	❏	❏
I used a writing rubric to evaluate my first draft.	❏	❏	❏
(Add something) _____	❏	❏	❏

_____

7

Health

" Health is worth more than learning. **"**

—Thomas Jefferson
Third president of the United States (1743–1826)

Connecting to the Topic

1 How are these people taking care of their health?

2 What do you do to take care of your health?

3 What would you like to start doing to take care of your health?

Exploring Ideas

 1 **Discussing Modern and Traditional Medicine** Look at the pictures below, and discuss them in groups of three. Answer the following questions:

1. What kinds of treatments are represented?

2. What do you know about these treatments?

3. What do you think of them?

▲ Both traditional and modern medical treatments come in many varieties.

2 **Discussing the Topic** Discuss the following questions in groups of three:

1. What do you do when you have a cold? Do you think modern treatments or traditional treatments are better for treating colds?

2. What traditional treatments do you know about? What do you think of them?

Building Vocabulary

3 **Using a Vocabulary Chart** Read the three short conversations below. Write the underlined words in the chart on page 112. Then complete the chart with words from your discussion in activity 2.

Doctor: What are your symptoms?

Patient 1: I have a <u>fever</u> and a <u>sore</u> throat.

Doctor: Does your throat <u>hurt</u> a lot?

Patient 1: Yes, it's very <u>painful</u> to eat.

Doctor: Sometimes tea with lemon and honey will <u>relieve</u> the pain <u>effectively</u>.

Patient 2: What is a good <u>treatment</u> for a headache?

Doctor: Aspirin is a very <u>safe</u> pain <u>reliever</u>.

Patient 2: I don't like to <u>take</u> medicine. I know a <u>healer</u> who uses <u>herbal</u> <u>teas</u>. They can also be good for <u>pain</u>.

Doctor: Maybe you should try <u>acupuncture</u>. Chinese doctors use it to <u>treat</u> many different problems.

Patient 3: Do you drink it? Is it an <u>herb</u>?

Doctor: No. An acupuncturist inserts <u>needles</u> into your body in different places.

Patient 3: It sounds painful. Is it <u>effective</u>?

Doctor: Yes, sometimes it works very well. Some people are completely cured by it.

Nouns	Verbs	Adjectives	Adverbs
symptoms			

ADDING SUFFIXES

When a suffix is added to the end of a word, it can change the word's part of speech.

Examples

The verb *teach* + the suffix *-er* = *teacher* (a noun)

The noun *friend* + the suffix *-ly* = *friendly* (an adjective)

Other common suffixes are *-ful, -ment,* and *-al*

Examples health<u>ful</u>, treat<u>ment</u>, medicin<u>al</u>

---

4 **Identifying Word Pairs** Look at the list of words in Activity 3. Find four pairs of words that are related. Complete the chart below.

Word		Suffix	New Word
treat	+	ment	treatment

Strategy

Using Idea Maps

In this chapter, you'll write a paragraph about traditional medicine. You can use an idea map to get started. An idea map is a kind of graphic organizer that you can use to generate and organize ideas for writing.

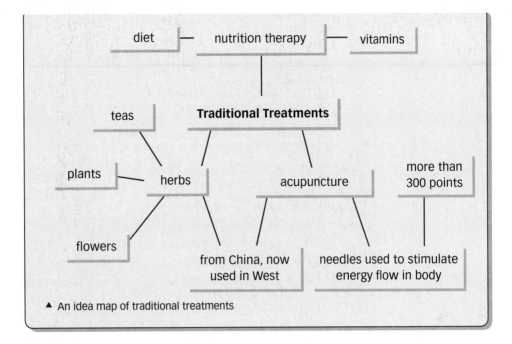

diet — nutrition therapy — vitamins

teas

Traditional Treatments

plants — herbs

acupuncture

more than 300 points

flowers

from China, now used in West

needles used to stimulate energy flow in body

▲ An idea map of traditional treatments

Organizing Ideas

5 **Creating a Graphic Organizer** Create an idea map for a paragraph about traditional medicine. Write the words *Traditional Treatments* in the middle of a piece of paper. Then write your ideas about the topic. Use the map above as a model.

6 **Choosing a Topic** Look at your idea map and decide which of the following topics you want to write about:

1. The different ways people use one kind of treatment.

2. The different treatments people use for one illness.

3. A short description of several different treatments you are familiar with.

4. A thorough description of one type of treatment.

7 **Brainstorming and Evaluating Ideas** Make a list of the ideas that you are going to use in your paragraph. Then evaluate your list. Use the checklist below to help you.

	Yes	No
1. The ideas are interesting. (If not, how can you find interesting details?)	❑	❑
2. I have enough information for one paragraph. (If not, where can you find more information?)	❑	❑

3. All the information is related to the topic.　❏　　❏
(If not, what can you cut out?)

Strategy

Writing a Good Topic Sentence
Remember that the topic sentence is the most general sentence in a paragraph. It usually comes at the beginning of the paragraph, but it doesn't have to. All the ideas in the paragraph should relate to the topic sentence. However, the topic sentence must tell the reader what the paragraph is going to be about, so it shouldn't be too general.

▲ Sometimes a combination of traditional and modern treatments can be effective.

Writing Topic Sentences

8 **Choosing the Best Topic Sentence** Circle the best topic sentence for a paragraph about each of the topics specified below.

Variety of herbal remedies used for different ailments

1. People often make teas with herbs to cure sore throats.

2. People use herbs to treat many different diseases.

3. I don't think herbs are as good as modern medicines.

Traditional treatments for colds

1. The best cures for the common cold might come from your own kitchen.

2. Lemon juice is a good traditional treatment for colds.

3. I had a horrible cold a year ago.

Different traditional treatments popular in the United States and Canada

1. One traditional treatment people in the United States and Canada often use is massage.

2. People in the United States and Canada often go to nutritionists.

3. Many people in the United States and Canada are using traditional treatments instead of modern medicine to treat a variety of health problems.

9 **Writing a Draft Topic Sentence** Look at the graphic organizer you created for your paragraph as well as your list of ideas. Write a draft topic sentence for your paragraph.

Developing Cohesion and Clarity

USING RESTRICTIVE RELATIVE CLAUSES

Good writers combine short sentences with relative pronouns to make longer, more natural-sounding sentences. The relative pronoun *who* is used for people. The relative pronoun *that* is used for people and things.

Examples

There are many people in the United States and Canada.

They are trying acupuncture.

There are many people in the United States and Canada <u>who/that</u> are trying acupuncture.

Aspirin is a very common medicine.

Aspirin is used to treat headaches and colds.

Aspirin is a very common medicine <u>that</u> is used to treat headaches and colds.

Notice that *who* and *that* always follow the noun they modify.

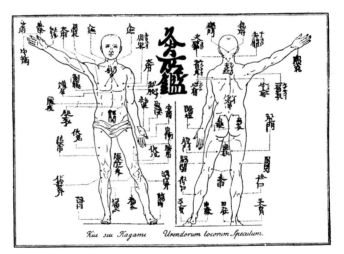

Kiu su Kagami.   Urendorum locorum Speculum.

▲ Chinese acupuncture chart

1 **Combining Sentences with Relative Pronouns** Combine the following sentences with *who* or *that.*

1. Acupuncture is an ancient treatment. This treatment was developed in China.

   Acupuncture is an ancient treatment that was developed in China.

2. She is a very skilled acupuncturist. She has cured many people.

3. People look for good acupuncturists. These people suffer from different diseases.

_____

4. Acupuncturists also use herbs. These herbs help treat health problems.

_____

5. Poor digestion is a common health problem. This problem can be treated with acupuncture.

_____

2 **Completing Sentences with Relative Clauses** Complete the following sentences with relative clauses that begin with *who* or *that*.

1. There are many traditional remedies _that can cure common health problems._

2. People _____ often use herbs to treat diseases.

3. I knew a woman _____

4. There are many plants _____

5. My friend goes to a doctor _____

6. My grandmother uses an herb _____

7. I know someone _____

8. There are some new medicines _____

9. I once used a traditional treatment _____

10. I once read a story about a man _____

USING TRANSITION WORDS AND PHRASES: *IN ADDITION, FOR EXAMPLE,* AND *HOWEVER*

Transition words and phrases help unify a paragraph. They can be used to add information, give examples, or introduce contrasting information. They often come at the beginning of a sentence and are followed by a comma.

Adding Information: *In addition*

In addition is similar to *and* and *also*. Use *in addition* when you are adding information that builds on or adds to the statements that come before it.

Example

The bark of certain trees can be used in traditional medicine. Herbalists make healing teas from tree bark. <u>In addition</u>, they can use certain barks to make a soothing cream to put on cuts and bruises.

Giving Examples: *For example*

Use *for example* when you want to give specific examples.

Example

Many people go to psychic healers. <u>For example</u>, my cousin went to a healer who cured his high fever with the touch of her hands.

Giving Contrasting Information: *However*

However is similar to *but,* but it is more formal. It is used to give contrasting information.

Example

Some psychic healers can cure many diseases. <u>However</u>, others just take people's money and don't help them.

Punctuation

Be careful not to use transition words to join two sentences with a comma.

These examples are correct:

He is a traditional healer. <u>However</u>, he uses some modern techniques.

He is a traditional healer; <u>however</u>, he uses some modern techniques.

This example is incorrect:

He is a traditional healer, <u>however</u> he uses some modern techniques.

---

3 Completing Sentences with Transition Words Complete the sentences below with *in addition*, *for example*, or *however.*

1. There are many Chinese acupuncturists in Canada. Many of them studied acupuncture in China and then immigrated to Canada. *In addition*_____, many Canadian doctors are now giving acupuncture treatments.

2. I often drink herbal teas when I am sick. _____, if I am very sick or have a fever, I take modern medicine.

3. Some people in California use many traditional treatments from various parts of the world. _____, they use remedies and treatments from China and India.

4. My grandmother often goes to an old lady who gives her very expensive treatments. _____, these treatments don't usually help her.

5. I use lemon juice for colds. I put it in a cup of warm water and drink it several times a day. _____, I take it for sore throats and fevers.

▲ Hot lemon tea with honey can help cure a cold.

4 **Writing Sentences with Transition Words** After each sentence, write another sentence that begins with *For example, In addition,* or *However.*

1. I don't use traditional treatments. *However, my sister thinks they are effective.*

2. Many herbal teas are good for digestion. _____
_____

3. She went to a nutritionist. _____
_____

4. Massage therapists can help you overcome headaches. _____
_____

5. It's important to eat healthful foods. _____
_____

GIVING REASONS AND SHOWING PURPOSE

In Chapter 5, you learned to use *because* to give reasons.

Example

My mother went to an acupuncturist <u>because</u> she didn't like to take medicine.

Because can also be used at the beginning of a sentence.

Example

<u>Because</u> my mother didn't like to take medicine, she went to an acupuncturist.

An infinitive (to + verb) can also show reason or purpose. This is called an infinitive of purpose. It means the same as *in order to.*

Examples

I drank herbal tea <u>to cure</u> my sore throat.
He gave me a massage <u>to help</u> my back.
The Chinese use acupuncture <u>to stop</u> pain.

When an infinitive of purpose or *because* comes at the beginning of a sentence, it introduces a dependent clause and should be followed by a comma.

Examples

<u>To stop the pain immediately,</u> the doctor gave me some medicine.
<u>Because I took the medicine regularly,</u> I couldn't feel my broken arm.

5 **Identifying Clauses that Show Reason and Purpose** Read the
paragraph below and answer the questions that follow.

Traditional Remedies

You don't have to spend a lot of money at a pharmacy to treat a cold because there are many inexpensive traditional remedies that are just as good as the modern ones. For example, my grandmother always advised us to drink honey and lemon juice in hot water to cure a cold. People who study natural medicine now say that lemon juice is good for colds because it kills germs, and honey contains natural elements that improve health. In addition, my mother used a natural remedy to help me breathe better when I had a cold. She put me in a room full of steam. Doctors still recommend this remedy. Because scientists haven't found any easily available medicine that kills viruses that cause colds, honey, lemon juice, and steam might be the most effective treatments available.

1. Underline the reason lemon juice is good for colds. What word introduces the reason? _____

2. Find a reason that comes at the beginning of a sentence. Circle it.

3. Find three infinitives of purpose. Draw two lines under them.

6 **Writing the First Draft** Write your paragraph about traditional treatments.
Remember to use *for example*, *because*, *to* + verb, *in addition*, *also, however* and
relative pronouns.

Part 3 | Revising and Editing

Revising for Content and Editing for Form

1 **Revising for Content** Read the paragraph on page 120, and make comments
and suggestions for changes on a separate piece of paper. Consider the following
questions:

1. Is all of the information relevant to the main idea of the paragraph?

2. Are transition words used to add information, give examples, and introduce
contrasting information?

Don't worry about misspelled words and other errors for now.

Amazing Traditonal Treatments

Some people can cure themselves of cancer with traditional treatments. I know a woman who cured herself of cancer by fasting. She didn't eat for one month, and then she slowly began to eat again. When she completed the fast she had completely fixed herself of cancer. I read about a man who cured his cancer using an traditional Chinese diet. As soon as he started the diet he begins to get better. Scientists don't have a modern drug to cure cancer.

▲ Medicinal herbs

USING EDITING SYMBOLS

You learned some editing symbols in Chapter 6. Below are more symbols your teacher may use.

wt This means *wrong tense*. The verb tense is incorrect.

ro You wrote a run-on sentence. A run-on sentence is an incorrect sentence that should be two sentences.

ww This means *wrong word*.

Example   *ww*
I like to swim to rest.
The author probably meant to say, "I like to swim to relax."

---

2 **Editing for Form** Now edit the paragraph above for form. Use editing symbols. Then rewrite the paragraph based on your comments and suggestions.

3 Editing Practice Rewrite the sentences below.

1. <u>m</u>any people in the Philippines drink herbal teas.

   Many people in the Philippines drink herbal teas.

2. The healer gave (to my friend) a foot massage.

   _____

3. Three years ago he h<u>ave</u> a stomachache. *wt*

   _____

4. His leg did not cure. *ww*

   _____

5. My friend didn't like to go to doctors, he went to a psychic. *ro*

   _____

Evaluating Your Writing

4 Using a Rubric Read the rubric below with your class. Then use the rubric to score your paragraph.

Score	Description
3 **Excellent**	■ **Content:** Paragraph presents enough information about the topic so that the reader has a very clear understanding of it. ■ **Organization:** Paragraph ideas are introduced by a topic sentence, and all sentences connect to this main idea. Related ideas are grouped together, and transitions are used effectively. ■ **Vocabulary:** Vocabulary is specific and used correctly throughout. ■ **Grammar:** Relative clauses are used correctly, ideas are connected with *in addition*, *for example*, *however*, and *because*, and infinitives of purpose are used to provide reasons. There are very few grammar mistakes, so meaning is clear. ■ **Spelling and Mechanics:** Sentences with relative clauses and transition words are punctuated correctly throughout. Paragraph includes very few spelling mistakes.

2 Adequate	■ **Content:** Paragraph presents information about the topic, but the reader may be left with questions. ■ **Organization:** Paragraph ideas are introduced by a topic sentence, and most of the sentences relate to it. Most related ideas are grouped together. ■ **Vocabulary:** Most vocabulary is used correctly. ■ **Grammar:** Relative clauses are used mostly correctly, some ideas are connected with *in addition, for example, however,* and *because,* and at least one infinitive of purpose is used to provide reasons. There may be some common grammar mistakes, but the meaning is clear. ■ **Spelling and Mechanics:** There may be some problems with the punctuation of relative clauses and sentences with transition words. There may be a few spelling mistakes.
1 Developing	■ **Content:** Paragraph does not present much information about the topic, or the topic is unclear. ■ **Organization:** Paragraph ideas do not connect to the topic sentence, or there is no topic sentence. Related ideas are not grouped together. ■ **Vocabulary:** Vocabulary is limited, and/or there are too many mistakes to understand the ideas. ■ **Grammar:** Relative clauses are not used or are used incorrectly. Transition words are not used or are used incorrectly. *Because* and infinitives of purpose are not used to provide reasons. Several grammar mistakes make meaning unclear. ■ **Spelling and Mechanics:** Paragraph includes many distracting spelling and/or punctuation mistakes.

5 **Peer Sharing** Exchange papers with another student, and read each other's work. Tell your partner one idea that you thought was interesting. If there is any part that you do not understand, tell you partner.

6 **Writing the Second Draft** Rewrite your paragraph using your rubric evaluation. Then give your paragraph to your teacher for comments and corrections. When your teacher returns your paper, ask him or her about any comments or corrections you don't understand.

Transition Words and Phrases

One part of the TOEFL® Internet-Based Test (iBT), writing section is called the "independent" task. A prompt (question) will instruct you to write for 30 minutes about a personal experience or a personal preference. Below are two sample independent writing prompts.

Sample Prompt 1

Some schools say that children should stay home if they think they're sick. This is supposed to stop the spread of disease. Other schools tell students to come unless they are extremely sick. Which do you think is a better system? Use specific examples or reasons to support your preference.

Sample Prompt 2

Describe a situation in which you were very sick. Support your response with specific details.

The first prompt gives you the opportunity to use "example" transitions, such as *for example, for instance,* or *as an example.* It also gives you a chance to use "listing signals" such as *first, next,* and *also.* The second prompt calls for "time" or narration transitions, such as five *years ago, then,* or *after that.*

Practice Using *example, listing,* or *time* transitions, respond to either Sample Prompt 1 or Sample Prompt 2. Before you write, set a timer for 30 minutes. You have that much time to plan, write, and revise your response.

Part 4 Expansion Activities

1 **Sharing Your Writing** With your class, make a short book of traditional treatments from around the world. Put all of your paragraphs in a binder. Illustrate the pages with drawings or pictures from magazines. Pass the book around the class, or give it to another English class to read.

2 **Writing About Health Treatments** Write about an illness or health problem you or a family member has or had. Describe the illness. How are/were you or they treating the problem? Was the treatment effective?

3 **Writing in Your Journal** Write in your journal for 10 minutes about one of the following topics:

1. Things to do to stay healthy.

2. How I keep my good health/What I do that is bad for my health.

3. The oldest person I know and his or her health secrets.

What Do You Think?

Analyzing the Differences Between Modern and Traditional Medicine
In what ways are modern and traditional medicines different? How are they the same? List them in the chart below. Use the features listed here and others you can think of. Discuss your answers with a partner, and give reasons for your choices.

- Is expensive/Is inexpensive
- Requires/Doesn't require formal training to practice
- Is dangerous/Is not dangerous
- Can be used to treat serious diseases/Can't be used to treat serious diseases
- Is natural/Is artificial
- Is controlled by the government/Isn't controlled by the government
- Can be used to cheat people/Can't be used to cheat people

Traditional Medicine	Modern Medicine

4 **Researching Traditional Health Treatments** Use a search engine to search the Internet for information about two different traditional treatments from two different parts of the world. Answer the questions below. Then share your information with the rest of the class.

1. What is the treatment?
2. What part of the world is it from?
3. What is it used to treat?

▲ Health food store

Self-Assessment Log

In this chapter, you worked through the activities listed below. How much did they help you to become a better writer? Check *A lot*, *A little*, or *Not at all*.

	A lot	A little	Not at all
I learned vocabulary for writing about remedies.	❏	❏	❏
I learned about common suffixes and how they change words.	❏	❏	❏
I used an idea map to generate and organize ideas.	❏	❏	❏
I learned to write a topic sentence for an informative paragraph.	❏	❏	❏
I practiced using restrictive relative clauses.	❏	❏	❏
I used transition words to connect ideas.	❏	❏	❏
I learned to give reasons with *because* and infinitives of purpose.	❏	❏	❏
I used a writing rubric to evaluate my first draft.	❏	❏	❏
(Add something) _____	❏	❏	❏

Entertainment and the Media

❝ No entertainment is so cheap as reading, nor any pleasure so lasting. **❞**

—Lady Mary Wortley Montagu
English letter writer (1689–1762)

Connecting to the Topic

1. What types of entertainment and media are pictured?

2. What types of entertainment do you like best?

3. What kinds of media do you read, watch, or listen to?

Exploring Ideas

1 **Categorizing Movies** Movies can be categorized by genre. Genre means *type*. Look at the photos and match them with the movie genres below.

action	drama	horror	fantasy
comedy	science fiction	musical	

1.

Star Wars

Genre: _science fiction_

2.

Chicken Run

Genre: _____

3.

Lord of the Rings

Genre: _____

4.

Evita

Genre: _____

5.

Cold Mountain

Genre: _____

6.

Scream

Genre: _____

7.

Rush Hour

Genre: _____

 2 **Discussing Movies** Discuss the questions below in groups of three.

1. What genre of movie do you like best?

2. What genre of movie do you like least?

3. What is your favorite movie? What genre of movie is it? Who are the stars of that movie? Who are the main characters? When and where does it take place?

Building Vocabulary

3 **Identifying Adjectives** Put a check mark next to the adjectives below that describe your favorite movie. Look up any words that you don't understand.

❏ action-packed	❏ funny	❏ realistic
❏ entertaining	❏ heartwarming	❏ sad
❏ exciting	❏ horrifying	❏ touching
❏ fascinating	❏ imaginative	❏ well-written
❏ frightening	❏ interesting	❏ well-directed

4 **Identifying Positive and Negative Adjectives** Look at the list of adjectives below. Put a check mark (✔) next to the positive characteristics and an *X* next to the negative characteristics. Put a question mark if you are not sure. Use your dictionary to help you. Discuss your answers with the class.

❏ ambitious	❏ fun-loving	❏ peaceful
❏ angry	❏ funny	❏ sexy
❏ brave	❏ gorgeous	❏ shy
❏ brawny	❏ handsome	❏ stocky
❏ brilliant	❏ hardworking	❏ stubborn
❏ childlike	❏ independent	❏ talented
❏ courageous	❏ innocent	❏ talkative
❏ crazy	❏ kind	❏ well-built
❏ egotistical	❏ loyal	❏ wicked
❏ evil	❏ ordinary	

5 **Choosing Adjectives** Who is your favorite character in your favorite movie? What is he or she like? Look at the list in Activity 4. Circle the adjectives that describe him or her.

6 **Writing Adjectives** List any other adjectives that describe your favorite character in your favorite movie.

_____ _____ _____

_____ _____ _____

_____ _____ _____

_____ _____ _____

Organizing Ideas

Strategy

Using a Story Web

In this chapter, you will write a one-paragraph movie review of your favorite movie. A movie review gives an overview of a film and includes genre, setting, plot, characters, conflict, and sometimes the film's resolution. In addition, a review includes the author's opinion of the movie.

You can use a story web, a graphic organizer that includes the elements of a story, to organize your ideas for your paragraph. When you create a story web, you should put the title of the movie in the middle, and draw six circles around the circle in the middle. The six circles should contain story elements: plot, setting, genre, character, conflict, and resolution. Then you can write notes about each element around these six circles.

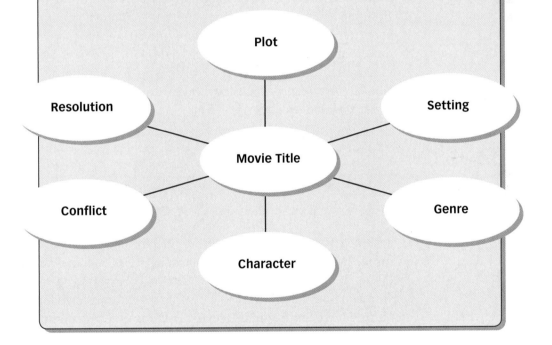

7 **Creating a Story Web** Using the story web above as a model, draw a story web for the movie you will write about. Write notes about your movie around each circle.

8 **Identifying Story Elements in a Movie Review** Circle and number the elements that you find in the movie reviews below.

1. title **3.** resolution **5.** conflict **7.** character
2. setting **4.** genre **6.** opinion

1 **Good Takes on Evil in Middle Earth**

The Lord of the Rings, my favorite book, recently became my favorite movie. This fantasy takes place in an imaginary place called Middle Earth. Many strange creatures live there. Some of them are good, and some are wicked. One group are innocent, peaceful creatures called Hobbits. A small Hobbit named Frodo inherits a very old ring when his uncle disappears. Gandalf, a kind wizard, says that the ring belongs to the evil Lord Sauron. He tells Frodo that he must take the ring to Mordor, an evil, far away place, and destroy it. The story is about Frodo's trip with three other Hobbits and a number of other creatures. They travel through mountains, snow, darkness, forests, and rivers. Along the way, they meet many dangerous creatures. The movie is quite frightening in places because the special effects are realistic. You'll have to see the movie to find out what happens. Does this brave group destroy the ring and save the world from darkness? Or do the evil lords win?

E.T.: An Unforgettable Story

One of my favorite movies is *E. T.: The Extra-Terrestrial,* a touching science fiction story about the friendship of a young boy and E. T., a creature from outer space. It takes place in the 1980s in a small American town. When E. T.'s spaceship leaves Earth without him, he meets Elliot, a boy who becomes his friend. Since E. T. is very homesick, Elliot decides to help him contact his friends. Because a group of scientists are searching for E. T. in order to study him, Elliot and E. T. have to escape from the scientists by bicycle. They go to the woods to meet the spaceship that will take E. T. home, and in a beautiful scene, they say good-bye. I found everything I like best about a movie in E. T.: wonderful characters, suspense, magic, and an ending that moved me to tears.

 9 **Discussing Movie Reviews** In a group of three students, discuss the story elements you identified in both reviews above. Discuss which ones are missing.

10 Choosing the Best Title If a movie review has an interesting title, the reader will want to read it. Look at the following titles. Which movies would you like to read about? Why?

1. *Incredible Voyage:* My Favorite Movie
2. *House of Flying Daggers:* An Unforgettable Experience
3. *Sam and Me:* A Good Movie

WRITING MOVIE TITLES

Titles of movies are italicized. If you are not able to italicize, then underline the title. All the important words in a title (of a movie, book, etc.) begin with a capital letter. Small words such as *and, in, a, the, to, at,* and *with* do not begin with a capital letter unless they are the first words in the title.

Examples
The Story of Qui Ju
Dona Flor and Her Two Husbands

11 Punctuating Movie Titles Punctuate the titles in parentheses and capitalize words that need capital letters. Don't include the parentheses in your answer.

1. You should see (the seven dwarfs), a classic Disney film.
   You should see <u>*The Seven Dwarfs*</u>*, a classic Disney film.*

2. The Chinese actor Chow Yung Fat was in (anna and the king).

3. The Italian movie (life is beautiful) won several awards.

4. Sandra Bullock starred in (while you were sleeping).

5. One of the most famous horror movies of all time is (the exorcist).

12 Writing a Title Write a draft title for your movie review on the line below.

Developing Cohesion and Clarity

> **Strategy**
>
> **Using Adjectives**
> One way to make a movie review interesting is to add adjectives that describe setting, characters, and events. Try to choose adjectives that are as specific as possible, and don't use the same adjective more than once in your paragraph.

1 **Completing Sentences with Adjectives** Look at the list of adjectives that describe movies on page 130. Then add an adjective to each of the sentences below.

1. *Star Wars* is a/an _____exciting_____ science-fiction movie.

2. *Dracula* is a _____ horror movie about a _____ vampire.

3. *Titanic* is a _____ love story about a couple on a sinking ship.

4. *Lord of the Rings* is a _____ fantasy about a _____ journey.

2 **Using Adjectives in a Sentence** Use adjectives to write a sentence about your favorite movie. Then underline the adjectives.

 3 **Writing Phrases with Adjectives** Make a list of some of your favorite movie characters. Look back at the list of adjectives on page 130. In a group of three students, write phrases describing those characters.

Example
E. T.—a magical visitor from another planet
Howard Hughes—an eccentric genius

USING APPOSITIVES

You can combine sentences using appositives. In Chapter 3, you learned that an appositive is a word or phrase that modifies a noun or a noun phrase and follows it directly. Appositives are set off from the rest of the sentence with commas.

Example
Han Solo is one of the heroes of *Star Wars*. He is a brave but egotistical pilot.
Han Solo, a brave but egotistical pilot, is one of the heroes of *Star Wars*.

---

4 **Identifying Appositives** Underline the appositives in the reviews of *E. T.: The Extra-Terrestrial* and *The Lord of the Rings* on page 132.

5 **Using Appositives to Combine Sentences** Combine the sentences below using appositives. Remember to use commas.

1. *Gone with the Wind* takes place in the south of the United States. It is a film about the U.S. Civil War.
    Gone with the Wind, a film about the U.S. Civil War takes place in the south of the United States.

2. In *Jurassic Park,* the dinosaurs seem real. It is a hair-raising thriller.

3. Cal Hockley is Rose's fiancé in *Titanic.* He is a rich but evil man.

4. *Cold Mountain* is a tragedy. It is a story about two lovers separated by war.

5. In *Shakespeare in Love,* Gwyneth Paltrow plays a woman who pretends to be a man. She is a famous American actress.

6 **Writing Sentences with Appositives** Write three sentences about your movie using appositives.

USING THE HISTORICAL PRESENT TENSE

Look at the paragraph about *E. T.: The Extra-Terrestrial* on page 132. Notice that it is in the present tense. We use the present tense to discuss actions and thoughts that occur in books and films. This is sometimes referred to as the *historical present tense*.

7 **Completing Sentences with the Correct Verb Tense** Complete the following paragraph with the correct form of the verbs in parentheses.

> *It's a Wonderful Life* _____ is _____ (be) a heartwarm-
> 1
> ing drama. In this movie, James Stewart _____ (play)
> 2
> an ordinary family man who _____ (live) in a small
> 3
> American town. When he is about to lose his business because of a seri-
> ous mistake, Stewart _____ (become) very depressed.
> 4
> He _____ (try) to jump off a bridge, but an angel
> 5
> _____ (show) him how important he _____ (be)
> 6   7
> to his friends, family, and community. He then _____ (decide)
> 8
> not to kill himself.

8 **Writing the First Draft** Write a one-paragraph review of your favorite movie. Be sure to include the following in your paragraph:

- title
- genre
- characters
- setting
- conflict
- opinion

When you write your review, you have to decide if you want to include the ending or resolution. Some people do not want to know the end before they see a movie. A review that gives away the ending is called a *spoiler*.

▲ Many people read movie reviews online.

Revising for Content and Editing for Form

1 **Revising for Content** Revise the following paragraph using appositives and removing any unnecessary information. Don't worry about misspelled words and other errors for now.

Spiderman 2: A Mild-Mannered Superhero

Spiderman 2 was the newest installment in the popular Spiderman series. Actor Tobey Maguire returned as the mild-mannered Peter Parker. We saw our hero having problems juggling his dual life as a college student studying economic theory and a superhuman crime fighter. His girlfriend Mary Jane Watson played by Kirsten Dunst, who also starred in many other movies this year, has found a new love and Peter considered giving up crime fighting in order to win her back. His plans were upset when he met his enemy Otto Octavius played by actor Alfred Molina. In this sequel, Parker's enemy was a many-armed maniac. Will Spiderman leave his superhero life or will he accept his fate and lose Mary Jane forever? Go see this entertaining movie and find out.

USING TWO OR MORE ADJECTIVES

Sometimes you may want to use more than one adjective before a noun. If you can say "and" between the two adjectives, use a comma to separate them.

Examples
E. T. is a friendly, lovable creature from outer space.
In *Million-Dollar Baby,* Clint Eastwood plays a bad-tempered, tough boxing coach.

When you want to use two contrasting adjectives, you can separate them with *but.*

Examples
In *Star Wars,* Han Solo is a brave but egotistical pilot.

2 **Punctuating Sentences with Adjectives** Look at the following sentences. Put a comma between the two adjectives.

1. *Chicago* is an entertaining energetic musical.

2. In *It's a Wonderful Life,* James Stewart plays a friendly hard-working man.

3. *Cold Mountain* is a sad disturbing movie.

4. *Spiderman* is a compassionate mild-mannered superhero.

3 **Adding *But* to Sentences with Adjectives** Put the word *but* between the contrasting adjectives in the sentences below.

1. *The Aviator* is the story of a wealthy~~but~~eccentric genius.

2. *Frankenstein* is the story of a destructive tragic monster.

3. *The Godfather* is about an evil loyal man.

4. *Million-Dollar Baby* tells the story of a poor determined young woman.

4 **Editing for Form** Edit the paragraph on page 137, changing the verbs to the historical present, correcting the punctuation, and making any other changes you feel are necessary.

Evaluating Your Writing

5 **Using a Rubric** Read the rubric below with your class. Then use the rubric to score your paragraph.

Score	Description
3 **Excellent**	■ **Content:** Paragraph describes a favorite movie so that the reader has a clear idea of the story. Paragraph contains elements of a movie review. ■ **Organization:** Paragraph ideas are introduced by a topic sentence, and all sentences connect to this main idea. Related ideas are grouped together, and the title makes the reader want to read the movie review. ■ **Vocabulary:** A variety of adjectives are used to effectively describe the movie elements. Vocabulary words are used correctly throughout. ■ **Grammar:** Historical present is used correctly throughout. Paragraph has very few common grammar problems so that the meaning is clear. Appositives are used correctly. ■ **Spelling and Mechanics:** Most words are spelled correctly, and punctuation of title, adjectives, and appositives is correct throughout.

2 **Adequate**	■ **Content:** Paragraph presents information about a favorite movie and contains most elements of a movie review. ■ **Organization:** Paragraph ideas are introduced by a topic sentence, but some ideas may not relate to it. Some related ideas are not grouped together. ■ **Vocabulary:** Some adjectives are used to describe the movie elements. Most vocabulary is used correctly. ■ **Grammar:** Historical present is used mostly correctly. Paragraph may have some grammar problems, but the meaning is clear, and appositives are used mostly correctly. ■ **Spelling and Mechanics:** Paragraph includes some spelling and/or punctuation mistakes.
1 **Developing**	■ **Content:** Paragraph does not present much information about a favorite movie, and most elements of a movie review are not included. ■ **Organization:** Paragraph ideas do not connect to the topic sentence, or there is no topic sentence. Related ideas are not grouped together. ■ **Vocabulary:** Vocabulary is limited, and/or there are too many mistakes to understand the ideas. ■ **Grammar:** Paragraph contains many grammar problems that are confusing to the reader. Appositives are not used or are used incorrectly. Historical present is not used correctly. ■ **Spelling and Mechanics:** Paragraph includes many distracting spelling and/or punctuation mistakes.

6 **Peer Sharing** Read another student's movie review. Have you seen this movie? If so, do you agree with the review? If you haven't seen the movie, does this review make you want to see it? Why or why not?

7 **Writing the Second Draft** Rewrite your paragraph using your rubric evaluation. Then give your paragraph to your teacher for comments and corrections. When your teacher returns your paper, ask him or her about any comments or corrections you don't understand.

Focus on Testing

The Historical Present Tense

In this chapter, you learned about the historical present tense. On the TOEFL® Internet-Based Test (iBT) this verb form is very useful in responses to integrated writing prompts. Remember that integrated writing prompts ask you to write about information from a reading and a lecture.

Examples

The reading <u>says</u> that the *Rambo* movies of the 1980s were some of the first modern action movies.

The lecturer <u>claims</u> that documentary movies are related to reality shows on television.

The talk <u>is</u> mostly about British actors.

Notice that the underlined verbs above are in the present tense. Other verbs in each sentence might be in the present or some other tense. However, in responses to an integrated writing prompt, the historical present is used if the subject of the verb is a word that means the *lecture, the reading, the lecturer,* or *the author.*

Practice Below is a sample response to the following prompt.

How does information from the lecture support the reading's claim that blockbuster movies often fail?

Circle the correct form of each verb in brackets.

Blockbuster movies are "big." They sometimes contain a lot of special effects, feature big movie stars, and cost a lot of money to make. The reading **(1)** [say, (says,) said] that the costs **(2)** [is, was, were] too high for a lot of movies in the past. The lecture **(3)** [add, adds, added] some examples from film history—such as *Waterworld* and *Heaven's Gate*—that **(4)** [lose, loses, lost] money. The author of the reading **(5)** [claim, claims, claimed] that special effects **(6)** [are, were, was] not always a good investment. Effects cannot save a movie that is poorly written or poorly acted. The reading passage also **(7)** [note, notes, noted] that many blockbusters are simply too long. The speaker also **(8)** [point out, points out, pointed out] that most audiences cannot comfortably **(9)** [sit, sits, sat] through a film that is two and a half or three hours long. He **(10)** [point to, points to, pointed to] *Heaven's Gate,* which **(11)** [is, was, were] originally three hours and 39 minutes long. The film studio eventually **(12)** [cut, cuts] it down to two hours and 29 minutes.

What Do You Think?

Analyzing How You Choose Movies

How do you choose the movies you see? What are the most important qualities in a movie to you? To find out, try the following activity.

Put a check (✔) next to the factors that are important to you in choosing a movie.

❑ director

❑ actors

❑ story

❑ music

❑ setting (where and when story takes place)

❑ special effects

❑ other: _____

Think about movies you have seen recently. Write the names of these movies in the chart below. Next to each movie, write your three most important reasons for choosing it. Some possible reasons might be:

- actors
- plot
- setting or time period
- special effects
- director
- music

Name of Movie	Reasons for Choosing a Movie		
	Most Important	Very Important	Important
1. *Titanic*	story	actors	special effects
2.			
3.			
4.			
5.			

When you finish, look at your list of movies and factors. Do you see any patterns in your choices? For example, do you have a favorite actor or director? Do you like movies about different times in history? Do you usually choose movies for the same reason(s)?

 Work with a partner. Exchange charts and look at your choices of movies. How are your choices and reasons similar or different? Did you see any of your partner's movies? Why or why not?

Write in your journal for 5 minutes about what you learned about yourself from doing this activity.

1 **Sharing Your Writing** Read three of your classmates' movie summaries. Discuss which movies you would like to see and why. If you have seen any of the movies, say whether you agree with your classmates' summaries.

2 **Discussing Movies** Think of a movie that you didn't enjoy. Make notes about why you didn't like it. Share your ideas with your classmates. Do people dislike movies for the same reasons? Do your classmates agree with your opinions?

3 **Writing in Your Journal** Write in your journal for 10 minutes about one of the following topics:

1. Violence in movies.
2. Why I like (or don't like) certain movies.
3. My favorite foreign film.

 4 **Looking Up Movie Reviews** Find out more about the movie that you wrote about or another movie that you are interested in. Do research online to find a positive review and a negative review. Then answer the following questions:

1. Why did the reviewer like or dislike the movie?
2. Do you agree with him or her? Why or why not?

▲ The movie *Be Cool* received good and bad reviews.

Self-Assessment Log

In this chapter, you worked through the activities listed below. How much did they help you to become a better writer? Check *A lot*, *A little*, or *Not at all*.

	A lot	A little	Not at all
I practiced categorizing movies by genre.	❑	❑	❑
I used a story web to organize ideas.	❑	❑	❑
I practiced identifying story elements.	❑	❑	❑
I learned about writing titles for movie reviews.	❑	❑	❑
I practiced using adjectives to describe characters and settings.	❑	❑	❑
I practiced using appositives.	❑	❑	❑
I learned to use the historical present tense.	❑	❑	❑
I used a writing rubric to evaluate my first draft.	❑	❑	❑
(Add something) _____	❑	❑	❑

_____

9

Social Life

" A free society is a place where it's safe to be unpopular. **"**

—Adlai Stevenson, Jr.
American diplomat and politician (1900-1965)

Connecting to the Topic

1. What kind of social gathering could this be?

2. Do you attend social events like this? Why or why not?

3. What are your favorite types of social events?

Exploring Ideas

1 **Discussing Interview Topics** In this chapter, you will write a paragraph about what one of your classmates has been doing in the past year. Join a group of three students, and make a list of topics to ask about in your interview.

hobbies _____   _____

_____   _____

_____   _____

2 **Writing Interview Questions** Write questions about the topics in Activity 1. Then add any other questions you'd like to ask.

3 **Preparing to Be Interviewed** You have prepared to interview a classmate. Now prepare for someone to interview you by making a list of the things you have done in the past year.

4 **Interviewing a Classmate** Use the questions from Activity 2 to interview a student about his or her life in the past year. Take notes on the information your partner gives you. When your partner interviews you, try to give him or her as much information as you can.

Building Vocabulary

5 **Completing Sentences** Complete the sentences below with the part of speech specified in the parentheses.

1. ___*Gardening*___ (noun) is Aziza's favorite hobby.
2. Marcos _____ (verb) to ice skate.
3. Blanca attended _____ (noun) when she had time.
4. Derek and his family took a _____ (adjective) trip.
5. Phichai has always been very interested in _____ (noun).
6. Kim _____ (verb) hiking in the mountains.
7. Katie has been taking _____ (adjective) lessons since she was five.
8. Victor has _____ (verb) many things this year.
9. Sam joined a _____ (noun).
10. Peter had so many _____ (noun) that he had almost no leisure time.

6 Adding Suffixes Complete the following chart by combining each verb and adjective in the first column with a suffix to form a noun. If necessary, use a dictionary to help you.

Verb/Adjective		Suffix		Noun
enjoy	+	-ment	=	enjoyment
accomplish	+		=	
responsible	+		=	
difficult	+		=	

Writing Topic Sentences

Strategy

Writing a Topic Sentence
The topic sentence for your paragraph should make a general statement about how the person you interviewed spent his or her leisure time last year. However, it should not be too vague or too specific. It should also make the reader want to read your paragraph.

7 Choosing the Best Topic Sentences Choose the best topic sentences for a paragraph about someone's life during the past year. Compare your answers with a partner's, and discuss your choices.

1. Raed Kamal has had little leisure time in the past year.

2. Reiko Suzuki has been married since June.

3. This year Paco Vega has been involved in so many activities he has felt like a juggler.

4. Hilda Bronheim learned a lot last year.

5. Li Yun Wen was a student last year.

6. During the past year, Ana Leone has had a full and happy life.

8 Writing a Draft Topic Sentence Write a draft topic sentence for your paragraph. Then show the sentence to the person that you interviewed.

▲ A juggler

Organizing Ideas

Strategy

Organizing Information in a Paragraph

There are many ways to organize your paragraph. You can:

- begin with activities that were important to the person, then move on to less important activities.
- write about the activities in chronological order with the earliest activities first.
- start with the activities the person spent the most time doing, and end with the activities the person spent less time doing.

These are just a few examples. No matter how you plan to arrange the activities in your paragraph, you should make sure that details about each activity are grouped together.

9 Discussing Order of Ideas Look at the following notes about one student's life. Work in small groups and decide on a method for organizing the ideas. Then number the notes in the order they would appear in a paragraph.

_____ had a surprise party for his parent's anniversary in March

_____ got married in June

_____ started playing chess in January

_____ played soccer with friends in the fall

_____ went to Miami for his honeymoon

_____ read biographies in the winter

_____ went biking with his wife in the spring

_____ practiced soccer almost every day

_____ they have been married for 25 years

10 Ordering Ideas for Your Paragraph Look at your notes from your interview and arrange them in the order you think you are going to write about them. Discuss the order with a partner.

WRITING A CONCLUDING SENTENCE

The final sentence in your paragraph can summarize how the person's year was, or it can look to the future.

Examples

All in all, Sandra has had a busy and fulfilling social life this past year.

Because he has spent the last year working really hard, next summer David plans to bike around Europe.

The following sentences are not good concluding sentences because they don't "wrap up," summarize, or look to the future. They introduce details that would be better suited to the body of the paragraph.

> Nancy has also learned to swim.
>
> Philip moved three times last year.
>
> Ken wanted to get a job in a bakery, but he couldn't find one, so he went to work in a restaurant.

11 **Identifying a Poor Concluding Sentence** Look at the sentences below. Which one would not make a good concluding sentence? Why?

1. In November, Raed's wife is going to have a baby, and then he will have much less leisure time.

2. With her new English skills, Sonia is hoping to get a better job.

3. Parvin says that it's a full-time job to take care of her kids, but she can't wait until they are in school and she can get a job that pays money.

4. Chatchai has also been learning to play tennis.

5. Next year, Satoshi is planning to return to Japan and use his English in his engineering work.

12 **Writing a Draft Concluding Sentence** Write a draft concluding sentence that you could use for your paragraph.

Part 2 Developing Writing Skills

Developing Cohesion and Clarity

USING THE CORRECT VERB TENSE
You can use the following chart to check your verb tenses.

Verb Tenses	Notes and Examples
Simple Present	A repeated, routine, or ongoing action in the present. **Example** Mina <u>studies</u> English in Austin, Texas.
Present Continuous	An action or situation that is in progress. **Example** Mina <u>is studying</u> and working right now.
Future	An action or state that will occur in the future. **Example** Mina <u>will study</u> in Texas next year.

Chart continued on next page

Verb Tenses	Notes and Examples
Simple Past	An action or a state that began and ended in the past. **Example** Mina <u>studied</u> in Texas last year.
Present Perfect	An action or a state (with verbs like *be, have, feel, know*) that began in the past and continues in the present. Often appears with *for* and *since* + time expression. Or an event that occurred in the past, but we don't know when. **Example** Mina <u>has known</u> her professor <u>for two years</u>. **Example** Mina <u>has studied</u> in Texas.
Present Perfect Continuous	An action that began in the past and continues to be in progress in the present; often appears with *for* and *since* + time expression. **Example** Mina <u>has been working</u> part time in the school cafeteria <u>since she arrived</u>. **Example** Mina <u>has been working</u> part time in the school cafeteria <u>for three months</u>.

1 **Choosing the Correct Verb Tense** Complete the following paragraph with the correct form of the verbs in parentheses. In some cases, more than one answer is correct.

Raed's life has been very busy this past year. He ___*has been going*___ (go) to the University of Beirut and _____ (work) part time since last fall. In addition, in February he _____ (join) a band, and he's _____ (work) hard with them ever since. However, music _____ (be) not Raed's only leisure-time activity last year. He _____ (be) also very involved in sports. In the spring, he _____ (try out for) a local football team. He _____ (make) the team and _____ (have) games every Saturday through the summer. Then in the fall he _____ (begin) learning to play tennis. He _____ (play) with his friend every week since then. In addition to playing sports and music, Raed _____ (spend) a lot of time traveling with his family in Saudi Arabia last year. He _____ (visit) his grandparents at least three times a month and _____ (attend) many family gatherings. All in all, Raed _____ (have) a busy but happy year.

▲ Raed kept very busy last year.

USING TRANSITION WORDS AND PHRASES: *HOWEVER, IN ADDITION,* AND *ALSO*

The transition words and phrases *however, in addition,* and *also* help unify a paragraph. *However* and *in addition* can begin a sentence, but *also* usually comes between the subject and the verb.

2 **Identifying Transition Words and Phrases** Find *however, in addition,* and *also* in the paragraph about Raed on page 150, and underline them. Then answer the questions below.

1. Which two expressions are used to give additional information?

_____

2. Which expression is used to give contrasting information?

_____

3. In the paragraph about Raed, is the expression in item 2 at the beginning or end of the sentence?

_____

4. Can the expression in item 2 be in another position?

_____

USING *IN FACT*

In Chapter 7 you learned to use *however* to give contrasting information. You can use *in fact* to introduce a concrete example that supports an idea or statement. Use a comma to separate *in fact* from the rest of the sentence.

Example
Raed has been very busy. <u>In fact</u>, he's been working at two jobs.

3 **Rewriting Sentences with *In Fact* and *However*** Add *in fact* or *however* to the second sentence in each pair below. Use commas where necessary.

1. Raed has been working very hard. He works from 8:00 in the morning until 9:00 at night.
Raed has been working very hard. In fact, he works from 8:00 in the
morning until 9:00 at night.

2. Raed has been working very hard. He still finds time to play soccer every week.

_____

_____

3. Raúl has been doing well, and he likes his English class a lot. He's been study-ing so much that he isn't sleeping well.

_____

_____

4. Raúl has been doing well in his English class. He went from level two to level four last month.

_____

_____

5. Patricia enjoys going to school. She doesn't like going at night.

_____

_____

6. Patricia has been exercising a lot. She now runs about 30 miles a week.

_____

_____

4 **Using Transition Words and Phrases in Sentences** Look at your notes and write two pairs of sentences for your paragraph. In the second sentence of each pair, use a transition: _however, in fact, also,_ or _in addition._

USING _SO . . . THAT_

You can combine two sentences to show cause and effect by using _so . . . that._

Cause	Effect
Raed has been busy.	He has felt like a juggler.
Raed has been <u>so</u> busy	<u>that</u> he has felt like a juggler.

5 **Combining Sentences with _So . . . That_** Combine the sentences below using _so . . . that._

1. Jane has been busy. She hasn't had much time to socialize.
   Jane has been so busy that she hasn't had much time to socialize.

2. Reiko was happy. She cried.

_____

3. Chi Wang has been working hard. He falls asleep in class.

_____

4. Nick has been happy here. He is seldom homesick.

_____

5. Sonia's daughter was sick. She had to take her to the hospital.

_____

▲ A doctor examines Sonia's daughter.

6 **Writing Sentences with** _So . . . That_ Write two sentences with _so . . . that_ for your paragraph.

7 **Writing the First Draft** Write your paragraph about a classmate. Remember to use transitional words and phrases.

Part 3 Revising and Editing

Revising for Content and Editing for Form

 1 **Revising for Content** Review the paragraph on page 154 for content. Discuss the following questions with a partner and make revisions:

1. Are the ideas organized well?

2. What order do they follow?

3. Do details follow general statements?

4. Is any information unnecessary?

5. Are transition words used well? Could any be added?

Don't worry about misspelled words and other errors for now.

A Great Year for Marta

Last year Marta Duarte had have a great time. Last June she graduated from a tourism development course in Mexico. She received a scholarship to study English and has been attending classes here at the University of Ottawa since September. marta is twenty-five years old. She went to New York in August. She's also been traveling in Canada and the United States. She love dance and went dancing at least two nights a week. She visits hotels to study the different management systems and has learned a lot. In fact, she says that one day in a hotel is better than ten days in a classroom. However, Marta hasn't spend all her time in Canada at work. She also find time to develop a close friendship with the manager of a big hotel here in Ottawa. She taught him to salsa dance. She is hoping to get to know him better.

▲ Marta Duarte had an exciting year.

USING CONTRACTIONS WITH 's

Contractions with 's can be used in different ways:

a contraction of subject + *be*	Harold's here. (Harold is here.)
a contraction of subject + *has*	Harold's gone home. (Harold has gone home.)

2 **Identifying 's Contractions** Write the sentences without contractions.

1. He's very satisfied with his life.

   He is very satisfied with his life.

2. She's moved three times this year.

_____

3. It's been cold and rainy.

_____

4. Recently she's been planning a party.

_____

5. It's difficult work.

_____

6. She's been getting dates from a computer dating service.

_____

3 **Spelling Present and Past Participles Correctly** Write the present and past participle forms of the words below. (For rules for adding -ing, see Appendix 1.)

	Present Participle	Past Participle
1. work	working	worked
2. begin		
3. study		
4. make		
5. find		
6. swim		
7. go		
8. travel		
9. come		
10. have		

USING CORRECT CAPITALIZATION

In your paragraph, remember to capitalize words correctly.
(See Appendix 2 for detailed rules.)

Capitalize months and days of the week.

Examples

July   September   Monday

Capitalize names of schools and businesses.

Examples

Lincoln Community College   Lucia's Bakery
University of Montreal   Interspace, Inc.

Capitalize languages

Examples

Japanese, Spanish, Thai, Arabic

4 **Capitalizing Words in a Sentence** Write the sentences below with correct capitalization.

1. Pablo has been studying computer science and english at northwestern college since january.

Pablo has been studying computer science and English at Northwestern

College since January.

2. Anna works as a dietician at randolph college.

_____

_____

3. In September, Van got a job as a mail clerk at a bank.

_____

_____

4. Tessa has been studying fashion design every tuesday and thursday evening.

_____

_____

5. Irena has been working with the jones plumbing company since the fall.

_____

_____

5 **Editing for Form** Edit the paragraph on page 154 for form. Correct verb tense, punctuation, and capitalization problems. Make any other changes to form that you feel are necessary.

Evaluating Your Writing

6 **Using a Rubric** Read the rubric below with your class. Then use the rubric to score your paragraph.

Score	Description
3 **Excellent**	■ **Content:** Paragraph describes what a classmate has been doing in the last year. ■ **Organization:** Paragraph ideas are introduced by a topic sentence, and all sentences connect to this main idea. Related ideas are grouped together, ideas are presented in a clear order, and transitions are used effectively. Paragraph includes an effective concluding sentence. ■ **Vocabulary:** Vocabulary is specific, varied, and used correctly. ■ **Grammar:** Verb forms are correct, and there are very few grammar mistakes so that meaning is clear. _So . . . that_ is used correctly. ■ **Spelling and Mechanics:** Most words are spelled correctly, and punctuation is correct. _'S_ contractions are used correctly.

2 Adequate	<ul><li>**Content:** Paragraph presents some information about a classmate's life in the last year, but the reader may have questions. Some irrelevant information may be included.</li><li>**Organization:** Paragraph ideas are introduced by a topic sentence, and most ideas relate to it. Some related ideas are not grouped together. Order of ideas may not be clear. Concluding sentence may not be effective.</li><li>**Vocabulary:** Vocabulary is varied, and mostly used correctly.</li><li>**Grammar:** Most verb forms are correct, but there may be some grammar mistakes. *So . . . that* is used correctly.</li><li>**Spelling and Mechanics:** Some distracting spelling and/or punctuation mistakes. *'S* contractions are used correctly.</li></ul>
1 Developing	<ul><li>**Content:** Writing does not present much information about a classmate's life in the last year.</li><li>**Organization:** Paragraph ideas do not connect to the topic sentence, or there is no topic sentence. Ideas are not presented in a clear order. There is no concluding sentence.</li><li>**Vocabulary:** Vocabulary is limited, and/or there are too many mistakes to understand ideas.</li><li>**Grammar:** Paragraph includes many grammar mistakes, making ideas confusing to the reader. *So . . . that* is not used.</li><li>**Spelling and Mechanics:** Many distracting spelling and/or punctuation mistakes.</li></ul>

7 **Peer Sharing** Give your paper to the person that you interviewed. Does he or she agree with all the information? Are all the facts correct? If not, correct them. Is there any important information you omitted? Can the person think of anything else that needs to be added?

8 **Writing the Second Draft** Rewrite your paragraph using your rubric evaluation. Then give your paragraph to your teacher for comments and corrections. When your teacher returns your paper, ask him or her about any comments or corrections you don't understand.

Focus on Testing

Managing Your Time on Standardized Tests

One of the greatest challenges in any writing test is to use your time wisely. The two writing tasks on the TOEFL® Internet-Based Test (iBT) are timed. For the independent writing task, you have 30 minutes. For the integrated task, you will read a short passage (3 minutes) and listen to a short lecture or conversation (2 to 4 minutes). Then you will have 20 minutes to respond to each prompt. You must plan, write, and revise your response within the time limit.

Below is one possible way to divide your time.

Task	Integrated Writing (20 minutes total)	Independent Writing (30 minutes total)
Thinking about the topic	2 minutes	3 minutes
Planning and making notes	2 minutes	3 minutes
Writing	14 minutes	21 minutes
Revising and editing	2 minutes	3 minutes

Practice Read the passage below and transcript of a lecture. Then set a timer for 20 minutes. In writing your response to the prompt, use the time guidelines above.

Reading

Lech Walesa, a former president of Poland, helped change Poland's entire system of government before becoming president. He was born in 1943 in the Polish city of Popowo. After serving for two years in the Polish army, he took a job as an electrician. He worked in a huge shipyard in a seaside city called Gdansk. The workers at this shipyard were angry because the government would not let them form their own union. Walesa led the workers in pointing out problems to the shipyard's managers.

A strike (a workers' refusal to work) by the shipyard workers took place in 1970. Over the next 20 years, Walesa and his co-workers tried to win freedom for the shipyard workers and for all of Poland. He became the first chairman of a new union called *Solidarity*. In 1983 he was given the Nobel Peace Prize for his efforts to bring peaceful change to Poland. The unpopular government of Poland was voted out of office in 1989, and Walesa was elected president in 1990.

Lecture

Lech Walesa rose to fame at an interesting time for Poland. The new Pope of the Roman Catholic Church was a Pole. Inspired by the pope, Polish people struggled to remove a harsh government. The Polish struggle was known all over the world.

Walesa's participation in the struggle got him into trouble. The strict Polish government arrested him several times in the 1970s. Walesa even temporarily lost his job at the Gdansk shipyard in 1976. When a stricter government took control in 1981, Walesa was locked up in a remote farmhouse for many months. He was finally released in 1982, but government spies kept following him wherever he went.

The former Soviet Union, which included Russia and several nearby regions, used to be a strong supporter of strict government in Poland. By 1989, however, the Soviet Union had decided not to use military force to influence other governments. Without the Soviet Union's soldiers, the Polish government could not stay in power. Poland held national elections, and Walesa came out as President of Poland.

Prompt: Using information from the reading and the lecture, describe how Lech Walesa influenced Poland's history.

Part 4 Expansion Activities

 1 **Sharing Your Writing** As a class, collect all the paragraphs to make a class newsletter about what everyone's done in the last year.

 2 **Guessing the Classmate** Remove your classmate's name from your paragraph. Give your paragraph to another classmate. Can he or she guess who you wrote about?

3 **Writing About Your Class** Write about what you and a group of people (your English class, for example) have been doing.

4 **Writing in Your Journal** Write about your leisure time activities in your journal for 5 minutes each day for a week. Then look back at your entries. Write for 5 minutes about what you have been doing.

What Do You Think?

Evaluating a Day in Your Life

How do you spend your time on a typical day? Do you spend time on things you really want to do? Find out by making a pie chart of your daily activities. Follow the steps below.

1. Draw a large circle on a piece of paper. Think of this circle as one day in your life.

2. Divide your circle into four quarters using dotted lines. (Each quarter = 6 hours of the day.)

3. Look at the questions below. Divide your circle to show about how many hours you usually spend on these activities. Draw lines and label the parts of your circle as in the example. There is no right or wrong way to do this. Everyone's life is different!

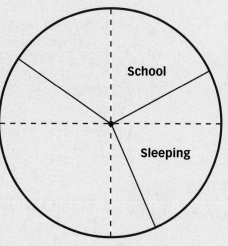
▲ A pie chart of daily activities

How many hours do you spend:
- Sleeping?
- In school?
- On homework?
- Working (if you have a job)?
- On other activities (use your own examples)?

4. When you finish, look at your pie chart. Are you happy with the way you are spending your time? Why or why not?

5. Draw another circle. This time, divide the circle to show how you would like to spend the day.

5 **Researching a Sport or Hobby** Find information on the Internet about a sport or hobby that you are interested in but know little about. Answer the questions below. Then share your information in groups of three.

1. Who participates in this sport or hobby? (for example, young people, adults, women)

2. Is it more popular in one part of the world than another?

3. Can you do it alone?

4. Does it require special equipment or training? If so, what kind?

5. Is it dangerous? If so, why?

Self-Assessment Log

In this chapter, you worked through the activities listed below. How much did they help you to become a better writer? Check *A lot*, *A little*, or *Not at all*.

	A lot	A little	Not at all
I interviewed a classmate.	❑	❑	❑
I learned about writing topic and concluding sentences.	❑	❑	❑
I learned methods for ordering information in a paragraph.	❑	❑	❑
I practiced using transition words and phrases.	❑	❑	❑
I learned to express cause and effect with *so . . . that*.	❑	❑	❑
I learned about different contractions with *'s*.	❑	❑	❑
I practiced spelling present and past participles.	❑	❑	❑
I practiced using correct capitalization.	❑	❑	❑
(Add something) _____	❑	❑	❑

10

Sports

❝Sports serve society by providing vivid examples of excellence.**❞**

—George F. Will
American newspaper columnist (1941–)

1. What sport is this?

2. Have you done this sport? Would you ever do this sport? Why or why not?

3. What sports do you like? Why do you like them?

Exploring Ideas

1 Categorizing Sports Look at the list of sports below. Join a group of three, and write the sports in the chart below. Some sports may fit into more than one category. Can you think of any other useful categories of sports? List them below the table.

baseball	ice skating	snowboarding
basketball	karate	soccer
bowling	kite surfing	swimming
fencing	rock climbing	tennis
golf	running	volleyball
horseback riding	scuba diving	water skiing
ice hockey	skiing	windsurfing

Winter	Dangerous	Water	Team

Other Categories: _____

_____

_____

2 **Choosing a Topic** In this chapter, you will write a comparison paragraph. Choose two sports or two types of sports that you would like to compare.

Building Vocabulary

 3 **Using a Vocabulary Chart** The following chart includes examples of vocabulary you can use to talk about sports. Work with a group of students and add to the chart. Discuss any words that you do not understand.

Nouns	Verbs	Adjectives
competition	challenge	athletic
competitor	compete	boring
danger	defeat	competitive
energy	lose	dangerous
fan	oppose	energetic
goal	participate	exciting
individual	play	individual
loser	race	noncompetitive
opponent	score	opposing
participant	win	safe
point		talented
race		tiring
score		winning
spectator		
talent		
team		
winner		

WORD FAMILIES

In the chart in Activity 3, some words are part of the same word family. Word families are groups of words that have similar meanings but may have different forms for different parts of speech. For example: *win*, *winner*, and *winning*.

My team will <u>win</u> the game. (verb)
We were the <u>winners</u>. (noun)
Marta scored the <u>winning</u> goal. (adjective)

4 **Finding Word Families** Find as many word families as you can in the vocabulary chart in Activity 3, and write them below.

opponent, oppose, opposing

_____   _____

_____   _____

_____   _____

_____   _____

Organizing Ideas

Strategy

Using Venn Diagrams
A Venn diagram contains overlapping circles and shows the similarities and differences between two things. The parts of the circles that do not overlap contain differences. The parts that do overlap contain similarities.

BASKETBALL   **BASEBALL**

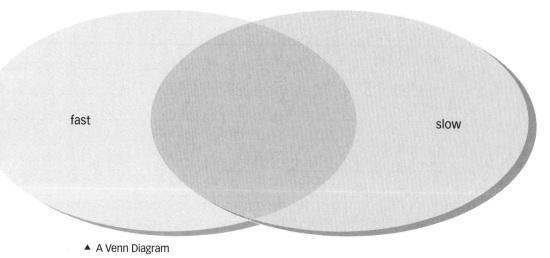

fast   slow

▲ A Venn Diagram

5 **Using a Venn Diagram** Look at the Venn diagram comparing basketball and baseball on page 166. Fill in the diagram with the phrases below. How are the sports the same? How are they different? Can you add any other characteristics?

play any time of year	played inside	team sport
play only in good weather	played outside	use ball and net
fast	played with a ball	use gloves and bats
slow		

▲ A basketball game

▲ A baseball game

6 **Creating a Venn Diagram** Create a Venn diagram. Write the names of the two sports you will write about in your comparison paragraph. Then fill the diagram with their similarities and differences.

Look at your diagram. Are there more similarities or differences? If there are more similarities, you should focus your paragraph on the ways the two sports are similar. If there are more differences, you should focus on the differences.

What Do You Think?

Finding Interesting Bases of Comparison
When two things seem similar, it can be interesting to read and write about their differences. Similarly, it can be interesting to discover the similarities in two things that seem different.

Your paragraph will be more interesting if you think of unusual bases of comparison. *Bases of comparison* are ways in which things can be compared. For example, you could compare basketball and baseball using the following bases of comparison: origin of the game, number of players, and where the game is played.

Discussing Bases of Comparison With a group of three people, think of the different ways that you might compare the sports listed below. For each pair, would you concentrate on differences or similarities?

badminton	baseball
cross country running	volleyball
judo	karate
karate	pole vaulting
horse racing	scuba diving

7 **Creating a Comparison Table** Look at your Venn diagram. Decide which points or bases of comparison you are going to write about. Write them in the left column in the comparison table below. Then use the other two columns to make notes on how the two sports or types of sports compare.

Bases of comparison	Sport 1	Sport 2
Pace of the game		

Beginning and Ending Your Paragraph

8 **Discussing Topic Sentences** With a partner, answer the following questions about each of the sample topic sentences below:

- What two sports or types of sports will the paragraph discuss?
- Will the paragraph be about similarities or differences?

1. Both swimming and diving take place in a pool, but they are very different sports.

2. Windsurfing and water skiing may seem very different, but they have many similarities.

3. The similarities between American football and World Cup football begin and end with the name.

4. Team sports teach the participants important lessons that individual sports don't.

9 Writing a Draft Topic Sentence Write a draft topic sentence for your paragraph.

WRITING A CONCLUDING SENTENCE

In your concluding sentence, you will give your opinion about the two sports or types of sports you compared. This type of concluding sentence often begins with a phrase that indicates opinion such as: *In my opinion, To my mind,* or *If you ask me.*

Examples

<u>In my opinion</u>, basketball is a much more exciting and satisfying game than baseball.
<u>To my mind</u>, people should stick to relatively safe sports such as swimming.
<u>If you ask me</u>, I'd always rather play a sport than watch it.

10 Writing a Draft Concluding Sentence Write a draft concluding sentence for your paragraph. Keep in mind that you can always revise it later.

Part 2 Developing Writing Skills

Developing Cohesion and Clarity

USING COMPARATIVES

Adjectives

To compare two things, use *-er + than* with one-syllable adjectives: cold<u>er</u> than, tall<u>er</u> than.
For two-syllable adjectives that end in *-y,* use either *-er* or *more:* <u>more</u> noisy, nois<u>ier</u>.
For adjectives of more than two syllables, use *more:* <u>more</u> expensive, <u>more</u> intelligent.
Certain adjectives are irregular: good—better, bad—worse, far—farther.

Spelling Notes

For one-syllable adjectives that end in a consonant, double the consonant and add *-er:*
   big—bigger   thin—thinner
For adjectives that end in *-e* simply add *-r:*
   wide—wider
For adjectives that end in *-y,* change the *y* to *i* and add *-er:*
   pretty—prettier   friendly—friendlier

Adverbs

You can compare two verbs using *more:* <u>more</u> slowly, <u>more</u> gracefully
Use *more* with almost all adverbs: happily—<u>more</u> happily.
Use *-er* with some irregular adverbs: fast—fast<u>er</u>, hard—hard<u>er</u>
For other irregular adverbs, use a different word altogether: well—better, badly—worse.

1 Forming Comparative Adjectives Write the comparative form of these adjectives and adverbs:

1. competitive _more competitive_
2. fast _____
3. exciting _____
4. athletic _____
5. sleepy _____
6. difficult _____
7. fat _____
8. slowly _____
9. good _____
10. well _____
11. tiring _____
12. boring _____
13. dangerous _____
14. safe _____
15. aggressively _____

WRITING ABOUT SIMILARITIES: USING *BOTH*

You can use *both* to show that two things are similar.

Before Nouns

Both skydiving and rock climbing are dangerous sports.

Before Adjectives

Skydiving and rock climbing are both dangerous.

Before Verbs

Skydiving and rock climbing both require a lot of experience.

As a Pronoun

Both are dangerous.

2 Combining Sentences with *Both* Combine the sentences using *both*.
Write the sentences three ways: with *both* before a noun, adjective, or verb, and as a pronoun.

1. Bowling is fun. Ping pong is fun.

   Both bowling and ping pong are fun.

   Bowling and ping pong are both fun.

   Both are fun.

2. Scuba diving is expensive. Skiing is expensive.

   _____

   _____

   _____

3. Baseball requires equipment. Football requires equipment.

   _____

   _____

   _____

4. Boxing can be dangerous. Wrestling can be dangerous.

   _____

   _____

   _____

5. Skiing is done in the winter. Snowboarding is done in the winter.

   _____

   _____

   _____

6. Competitive sports are on TV. Team sports are on TV.

   _____

   _____

   _____

WRITING ABOUT DIFFERENCES: USING *BUT*

Use *but* to combine two parallel sentences with contrasting ideas. If the resulting sentence includes two independent clauses, put a comma before *but.*

Examples
Scuba diving requires expensive equipment. Running doesn't require expensive equipment.
Scuba diving requires expensive equipment, <u>but</u> running doesn't.

Volleyball is a team sport. Tennis isn't a team sport.
Volleyball is a team sport, <u>but</u> tennis isn't.

But can also be used to combine sentences that are not parallel.

Examples

Scuba diving requires expensive equipment. You don't have to buy it.
Scuba diving requires expensive equipment, <u>but</u> you don't have to buy it.

Individual sports can be fun. They are quite lonely.
Individual sports can be fun, <u>but</u> they are quite lonely.

▲ Scuba diving requires expensive equipment.

Using *However*

You can use *however* to introduce a contrasting idea.

Compare the punctuation in the pairs of combined sentences below. When do you use a comma? When do you use a semicolon?

Examples

Skiing is a dangerous sport. Skiing is exciting.
Skiing is a dangerous sport. <u>However</u>, it is very exciting.
Skiing is a dangerous sport; <u>however</u>, it is very exciting.

Many people think that bowling is boring. I enjoy it.
Many people think that bowling is boring. <u>However</u>, I enjoy it.
Many people think that bowling is boring; <u>however</u>, I enjoy it.

---

3 **Rewriting Sentences with *But* and *However*** Rewrite the sentences below. Change *but* to *however* and *however* to *but*. Change the punctuation as necessary.

1. Golf may be interesting to some people, but I think it's incredibly silly.
   Golf may be interesting to some people; however, I think it's incredibly silly.

2. Ice hockey can be very violent. However, it's also extremely exciting to watch.

3. When I was a child, I loved to participate in sports, but now I prefer to be a spectator.

4. I love going to football games; however, I always feel bad if my team loses.

_____

_____

5. I admire windsurfers. But I'd be too scared to try windsurfing.

_____

_____

6. Skiing looks like fun, but I never go because I hate speed and I'm afraid of heights.

_____

_____

4 **Rewriting Sentences Using *Both*, *But*, and *However*** Add the words in parentheses to the sentences. Sometimes you will have to combine the sentences. Sometimes you will just need to add the new word(s).

1. Team sports are fun. Individual sports are fun.
They are different in two important ways. (both, however)

   Both team and individual sports are fun; however, they are

   different in two important ways.

2. The first difference is that you can do individual sports alone. You don't need anyone to go cycling or running. A football player can't just pick up a ball and decide to play. (but)

   _____

   _____

3. Volleyball requires opponents. Baseball requires opponents. (both)

   _____

   _____

4. Ice skating requires no teammates. Rock climbing requires no teammates. (both)

   _____

   _____

5. Basketball and soccer require teammates. You can practice basketball and soccer on your own. (both, however)

   _____

   _____

5 **Writing the First Draft** Write your paragraph using the information from Part 1. Remember to start with a topic sentence that introduces the main idea of your paragraph. Don't forget to state your opinion in your concluding sentence. Use the following:

- comparative adjectives and adverbs
- *both*
- *but*
- *however*

Part 3 Revising and Editing

Revising for Content and Editing for Form

1 **Revising for Content** Read the paragraph on page 175, and choose the best topic sentence from the three below. Write it on the lines provided. Then combine sentences where it is appropriate.

1. Individual sports and team sports are good for the people who participate in them.

2. Team sports are much more interesting than individual sports.

3. Both team and individual sports are fun. However, they are different in two important ways.

▲ Rockclimbing is a challenging individual sport.

Don't worry about misspelled words and other errors for now.

_____

_____

The first difference is that you can do individual sports alone. You do not need anyone to go cycling. You do not need anyone to go running. And a tennis player cannot just pick up a racket and decide to play, either. A tennis player needs an opponent. Team sports such as volleyball or baseball need even more people. To participate in these sports, you have to have two opposing teams. They require space to play too. Soon you need schedules, teams, and uniforms. Team sports are much formaler than individual sports. However, there is also another major difference between team and individual sports: the score. When I go ice skating, no one judges my performance. There are no losers in rock climbing. One team in a football game is the winner.

▲ Ice skating can be done individually or with a partner.

One team in a football game is the loser. Competition can make even an informal game of ping pong stressful. In my opinion, sports should be fun. Team sports create a lot of work and a lot of stress.

2 **Editing for Form** Edit the paragraph above for form. Look for problems with connecting words and comparative structures. Make any other changes you feel are necessary.

Evaluating Your Writing

3 **Using a Rubric** Read the rubric below with your class. Then use the rubric to score your paragraph.

Score	Description
3 **Excellent**	■ **Content:** Paragraph compares two sports, states preference, and includes interesting bases of comparison. ■ **Organization:** Paragraph ideas are introduced by a topic sentence, and related ideas are grouped together. ■ **Vocabulary:** Vocabulary is varied and used correctly. ■ **Grammar:** Verb forms are correct, and comparative adjectives are used correctly. ■ **Spelling and Mechanics:** Most words are spelled correctly, and punctuation is correct.
2 **Adequate**	■ **Content:** Paragraph describes two sports and states preference. It may not include interesting bases of comparison. ■ **Organization:** Paragraph ideas are introduced by a topic sentence. All related ideas are not grouped together. ■ **Vocabulary:** Vocabulary is somewhat varied. Some words may be used incorrectly. ■ **Grammar:** Most verb forms are correct. Comparative adjectives are mostly used correctly. ■ **Spelling and Mechanics:** There are some distracting spelling and/or punctuation mistakes.
1 **Developing**	■ **Content:** Writing does not present much information about two sports or includes unimportant or unrelated details. ■ **Organization:** Paragraph ideas do not connect to the topic sentence, or there is no topic sentence. Related ideas are not grouped together. ■ **Vocabulary:** Vocabulary is limited, and/or there are too many mistakes to understand the ideas. ■ **Grammar:** Paragraph includes many grammar mistakes that make ideas confusing to the reader. Comparative adjectives are not used or are used incorrectly. ■ **Spelling and Mechanics:** Many distracting spelling and/or punctuation mistakes.

4 **Peer Sharing** Let a partner read your paragraph. Ask your partner to give two reasons he or she agrees or disagrees with your opinion.

5 **Writing the Second Draft** Rewrite your paragraph using your rubric evaluation. Then give your paragraph to your teacher for comments and corrections. When your teacher returns your paper, ask him or her about any comments or corrections you don't understand.

Focus on Testing

Describing Differences

In this chapter, you learned about using *but* and *however* to express differences. Independent writing prompts on the TOEFL® Internet-Based Test (iBT) often ask you to write about the differences between the ideas in a reading and those in a lecture.

Practice The table below illustrates differences between two sports: skiing and snowboarding. Write one sentence to express each difference. The first one is done for you as an example.

Basis of Comparison	Skiing	Snowboarding
Equipment	two narrow boards	one wide board
Age of Sport	hundreds of years old	began in the 1960s
Origin	no inventor is known	invented by Sherman Poppen of Muskegon, Michigan
Status in 1970s	allowed on hills at commercial resorts	not allowed on hills at commercial resorts
Dress of Participants in 1970s	expensive special clothing	ordinary, inexpensive clothes
Age of Participants Now	many over 30	not many over 30

1. *A skier uses two narrow boards, but a snowboarder uses only a single wide one.*

2. _____

3. _____

4. _____

5. _____

_____

6. _____

_____

Part 4   Expansion Activities

 1 Discussing Sports and Hobbies with a Partner Work with a partner. Find a sport or activity that only you do. Then find a sport or activity that only your partner does. Choose three bases of comparison, and discuss how the sports are similar and different.

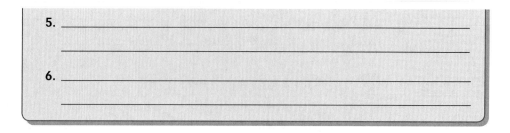

▲ Croquet is a popular lawn sport.

2 Writing About a Sport Think of a sport or activity that is not part of the Olympic Games. Write a paragraph describing why you think the sport should be played at the Olympics. Share your ideas with the class.

 3 Writing About Sports Celebrities Work with a group of three students. Choose two sports celebrities to compare. Find three interesting bases of comparison, and write a paragraph about the sports stars' similarities and differences. Share your ideas with the class.

4 Writing in Your Journal Write for 10 minutes about one of the following topics:

1. Compare two people that you know. Find three interesting bases of comparison. Then write as much as you can about how these two people compare.

2. Compare two places that you have been. Find three interesting bases of comparison. Then write as much as you can about how these two places compare.

5 **Researching the Olympic Games** Research the Olympic Games on the Internet. Find out how they have changed since they were restarted in 1896. You can compare the ancient Olympics in Greece to the modern Olympics or compare the Olympics of 50 years ago with the Olympics of today.

Self-Assessment Log

In this chapter, you worked through the activities listed below. How much did they help you to become a better writer? Check *A lot*, *A little*, or *Not at all*.

	A lot	A little	Not at all
I categorized sports.	❑	❑	❑
I practiced finding bases of comparison.	❑	❑	❑
I learned to use a Venn diagram.	❑	❑	❑
I practiced using a comparison table.	❑	❑	❑
I practiced writing topic and concluding sentences.	❑	❑	❑
I practiced using comparative adjectives and adverbs.	❑	❑	❑
I learned to use *both* to write about similarities.	❑	❑	❑
I learned to use *but* and *however* to write about differences.	❑	❑	❑
(Add something) _____	❑	❑	❑

_____

Appendix 1

Spelling Rules for Adding Endings

Endings That Begin with Vowels (-*ed*, -*ing*, -*er*, -*est*)

1. For words ending in silent *e*, drop the *e* and add the ending.

   lik**e** ⟶ lik**ed**   mak**e** ⟶ mak**ing**   saf**e** ⟶ saf**er**   fin**e** ⟶ fin**est**

2. For one-syllable words ending in a single vowel and a single consonant, double the final consonant, and add the ending.

   ba**t** ⟶ bat**ted** ru**n** ⟶ run**ning**   fa**t** ⟶ fat**ter**   ho**t** ⟶ hot**test**

3. Don't double the final consonant when the word has two final consonants or two vowels before a final consonant.

   pi**ck** ⟶ pic**ked**   si**ng** ⟶ sing**ing**   cle**an** ⟶ clea**ner**   co**ol** ⟶ coo**lest**

4. For words of two or more syllables that end in a single vowel and a single consonant, double the final consonant if the stress is on the final syllable.

   ref**er** ⟶ refer**red**   beg**in** ⟶ begin**ning**   beg**in** ⟶ begin**ner**

5. For words of two or more syllables that end in a single vowel and a single consonant, make no change if the stress is not on the final syllable.

   trav**el** ⟶ trave**led**   trav**el** ⟶ trave**ling**
   trav**el** ⟶ trave**ler**   yell**ow** ⟶ yellow**est**

6. For words ending in a consonant and *y*, change the *y* to *i* and add the ending unless the ending begins with *i*.

   stud**y** ⟶ stud**ied**   dirt**y** ⟶ dirt**ier**   sunny ⟶ sunn**iest**
   stud**y** ⟶ stud**ying**   hurry ⟶ hurr**ying**

7. For words ending in a vowel and *y*, make no change before adding the ending.

   play ⟶ play**ed**   stay ⟶ stay**ing**   play ⟶ play**er**   gray ⟶ gray**est**

Endings That Begin with Consonants (-*ly*, -*ment*)

1. For words ending in a silent *e*, make no change when adding endings that begin with consonants.

   fine ⟶ fine**ly**   state ⟶ state**ment**

2. For words ending in a consonant and *y*, change the *y* to *i* before adding the ending.

   hap**py** ⟶ happ**ily**   mer**ry** ⟶ merr**iment**

Adding a Final *s* to Nouns and Verbs

1. Generally, add the *s* without making changes.

   sit ⟶ sit**s**   dance ⟶ dance**s**   play ⟶ play**s**   book ⟶ book**s**

2. If a word ends in a consonant and *y*, change the *y* to *i* and add *es*.

   mar**ry** ⟶ marr**ies**   stu**dy** ⟶ stud**ies**   cher**ry** ⟶ cherr**ies**

3. If word ends in *ch*, *s*, *sh*, *x*, or *z*, add *es*.

   chur**ch** ⟶ church**es**   ca**sh** ⟶ cash**es**   fi**zz** ⟶ fizz**es**
   bo**ss** ⟶ boss**es**   mi**x** ⟶ mix**es**

4. For words ending in *o*, sometimes add *es* and sometimes add *s*.

   tomat**o** ⟶ tomato**es**   potat**o** ⟶ potato**es**
   pian**o** ⟶ piano**s**   radi**o** ⟶ radio**s**

5. For words ending in *f* or *fe*, generally drop the *f* or *fe* and add *ves*.

   hal**f** ⟶ hal**ves**   kni**fe** ⟶ kni**ves**

   Exceptions: sa**fe** ⟶ safe**s**   roo**f** ⟶ roof**s**

Appendix 2

Capitalization Rules
First Words

1. Capitalize the first word of every sentence.

   They live near my house.   **W**hat is it?

2. Capitalize the first word of a quotation that is a full sentence.

   He said, "**M**y name is Paul."   Jenny asked, "**W**hen is the party?"

Personal Names

1. Capitalize the names of people including initials and titles.

   Mrs. **J**ones   **M**ohandas **G**andhi   **J**ohn **F**. **K**ennedy

2. Capitalize family words if they appear alone or followed by a name.

   Let's go, **D**ad.   Where's **G**randma?   She's at **A**unt **L**ucy's.

3. Don't capitalize family words with a possessive pronoun or article.

   my **u**ncle   her **m**other   our **g**randparents   an **a**unt

4. Capitalize the pronoun *I*.

   I have a book.   She's bigger than **I** am.

5. Capitalize the names of nationalities, races, peoples, and religions.

Japanese   **A**rab   **A**sian   **C**hicano   **M**uslim

6. Generally, don't capitalize occupations.

I am a **s**ecretary.   She wants to be a **l**awyer.

Place Names

1. Capitalize the names of countries, states, provinces, and cities.

Lebanon   **N**ew **Y**ork   **Q**uebec   **I**stanbul

2. Capitalize the names of oceans, lakes, rivers, islands, and mountains.

the **A**tlantic **O**cean   **L**ake **C**omo   the **N**ile **R**iver
Maui   **M**t. **A**rarat

3. Capitalize the names of geographical areas.

the **S**outh   the **M**iddle **E**ast   **A**frica   **A**ntarctica

4. Don't capitalize directions if they aren't names of geographical areas.

He lives **e**ast of Toronto.   We walked **s**outhwest.

5. Capitalize names of schools, parks, buildings, and streets.

the **U**niversity of **G**eorgia   **C**entral **P**ark
the **S**ears **B**uilding   **O**xford **R**oad

Time Words

1. Capitalize names of days and months.

Monday   **F**riday   **J**anuary   **M**arch

2. Capitalize names of holidays and historical events.

Independence **D**ay   **W**orld **W**ar II

3. Don't capitalize names of seasons.

spring   **s**ummer   **f**all   **w**inter

Titles

1. Capitalize the first word and all important words of titles of books, magazines, newspapers, songs, and articles.

Interactions   *The New York Times*   "Traveling in Egypt"

2. Capitalize the first word and all important words in titles of movies, plays, radio programs, and television programs.

The Matrix   *The Tempest*   *News Roundup*   *The Simpsons*

3. Don't capitalize articles (*a, an, the*) conjunctions (*but, and, or*) or short prepositions (*of, with, in, on, for*) unless they are the first word of a title.
The Life of Pi   *War and Peace*   *Death of a Salesman*

Names of Organizations

1. Capitalize the names of organizations, government groups, and businesses.

   International **S**tudent **A**ssociation   the **S**enate   **G**oogle™

2. Capitalize brand names, but do not capitalize the names of the product.

   IBM™ computer   **T**oyota™ truck   **K**ellogg's™ cereal

Other

1. Capitalize the names of languages.

   Arabic   **S**panish   **T**hai   **J**apanese

2. Don't capitalize school subjects unless they are the names of languages or are followed by a number.

   geometry   **m**usic   **E**nglish   **W**riting 101   **H**istory 211

Appendix 3

Punctuation Rules

Period

1. Use a period after a statement or command.

   We are studying English.   Open your books to Chapter 3.

2. Use a period after most abbreviations.

   Mr.   Ms.   Dr.   Ave.   etc.

3. Use a period after initials.

   H. G. Wells   Dr. H. R. Hammond

Question Mark

1. Use a question mark after (not before) questions.

   Where are you going?   Is he here yet?

2. In a direct quotation, the question mark goes before the quotation marks.

   He asked, "What's your name?"

Exclamation Point

Use an exclamation point after exclamatory sentences or phrases.

Let the students vote!   Be quiet!   Wow!

*In academic writing, exclamation points are very rare.

Comma

1. Use a comma before a conjunction (*and*, *or*, *so*, *but*) that separates two independent clauses.

   She wanted to work, so she decided to study English.
   He wasn't happy in his apartment, but he didn't have the money to move.

2. Don't use a comma before a conjunction that separates two phrases that aren't complete sentences.

   She worked in the library and studied at night.
   Do you want to go to a movie or stay home?

3. Use a comma after an introductory phrase (generally, if it is five or more words long).

   During the long summer vacation, I decided to learn Chinese.
   After a beautiful wedding ceremony, they had a reception in her mother's home.

   If you want to write well, you should practice often.

4. Use a comma to separate interrupting expressions from the rest of a sentence.

   Do you know, by the way, what time dinner is?
   Many of the students, I found out, stayed on campus during the holidays.

5. Use a comma after transition words and phrases.

   In addition, he stole all her jewelry.
   Common transitional words and phrases are:

also	for this reason	in addition	on the other hand
besides	for instance	in fact	similarly
consequently	furthermore	moreover	therefore
for example	however	nevertheless	

6. Use a comma to separate names of people in direct address from the rest of a sentence.

   Jane, have you seen Paul?
   We aren't sure where he is, Ms. Green.

7. Use a comma after *yes* and *no* in answers.

   Yes, he was here a minute ago.
   No, I haven't.

8. Use a comma to separate items in a series.

   We have coffee, tea, and milk.
   He looked in the refrigerator, on the shelves, and in the cupboard.

9. Use a comma to separate an appositive from the rest of a sentence.

   Mrs. Sampson, his English teacher, gave him a bad grade.
   Would you like to try a taco, a delicious Mexican food?

10. If a date or address has two or more parts, use a comma after each part.

I was born on June 5, 1968.
The house at 230 Seventh Street, Miami, Florida is for sale.

11. Use a comma to separate contrasting information from the rest of the sentence.

It wasn't Jamila, but Fatima, who was absent.
Bring your writing book, not your reading book.

12. Use a comma to separate quotations from the rest of a sentence.

He asked, "What are we going to do?"
"I didn't have enough money," she explained.

13. Use a comma to separate two or more adjectives that each modify the noun alone.

She was an intelligent, beautiful actress. (*intelligent* and *beautiful* actress)
Eat those delicious green beans. (*delicious* modifies *green beans*)

14. Use a comma to separate nonrestrictive clauses from the rest of a sentence. A nonrestrictive clause gives more information about the noun it describes, but it isn't needed to identify the noun. Clauses after proper names are nonrestrictive and require commas.

It's a Wonderful Life, which is often on television at Christmas time, is my favorite movie.
James Stewart, who plays a depressed man thinking of ending his life, received an Academy Award for his performance.

Semicolons

1. A semicolon is often an alternative to a period. Use a semicolon between two sentences that are very closely related.

I'm sure Dan is at home; he never goes out on school nights.

2. Use a semicolon before transition words and phrases such as *however, therefore, nevertheless, furthermore, for example, as a result, that is,* and *in fact.*

Malaria is a major health problem around the world; however, some progress is being made in developing low-cost treatments for it.

Quotation Marks

1. Use quotation marks at the beginning and end of exact quotations. Other punctuation marks go before the end quotation marks.

He said, "I'm going to Montreal."
"How are you traveling to France?" he asked.

2. Use quotation marks before and after titles of works that appear within larger works: short stories, articles, and songs. Periods and commas go before the final quotation marks.

My favorite song is "Let it Be."

Apostrophes

1. Use apostrophes in contractions.

don't   it's*   we've   they're

*Notice the difference between: It's hot. (*It's* is a contraction of *it is*.)
The dog is hurt. Its leg is broken. (*Its* is possessive.)

2. Use an apostrophe to make possessive nouns.

Singular: Jerry's   my boss's
Plural: the children's   the Smiths'

Underlining and Italicizing

The tiles of books, magazines, newspapers, plays, television programs, and movies should be italicized. If italicizing is not possible because you are writing by hand, underline instead.

I am reading *One Hundred Years of Solitude*.
Did you like the movie *Crash*?

Appendix 4

A List of Noncount Nouns

Food

bread, butter, cheese, chicken*, chocolate, coffee,* cream, fish,* flour, fruit, ice cream,* juice, meat, milk, rice, salt, spaghetti, sugar, tea

Activities and Sports

baseball,* chess, dance,* skating, soccer, tennis

* These nouns have both count and noncount uses. They are noncount when they refer to the item in general. They are count when they refer to a particular item.

I love chicken. (the meat)
The farmer raised twenty chickens. (the animals)
Coffee is delicious. (the drink)
Can I have a coffee please? (a cup of coffee)

Natural Phenomena

Weather:	rain, snow, sunshine, thunder, wind
Gases:	air, hydrogen, nitrogen, oxygen
Minerals:	copper, gold, iron, silver, steel
Materials:	dirt, dust, grass, ice, land, oil, sand, water

Emotions and Qualities**

ambition, anger, courage, fear, freedom, happiness, hatred, honesty, justice, loneliness, love, joy, pride

Social Issues**

abortion, crime, democracy, divorce, freedom, hunger, nuclear power, peace, pollution, poverty

Mass Nouns (Composed of Dissimilar items)

change, clothing, fruit, equipment, furniture, information, jewelry, luggage, mail, machinery, makeup, medicine, money, noise, scenery, technology, transportation, vocabulary

Subjects

art, economics, history, humanities, physics

Miscellaneous

advice, business, fun, glass, homework, knowledge, information, insurance, life, nature, news, paint, publicity, reality, research, sleep, time, traffic, trouble, tuition, work

** Most emotions, qualities, and social issue nouns can also function as count nouns: a strong ambition, a deep hatred, a terrible crime, a young democracy

Appendix 5

Subordinating Conjunctions

Subordinating conjunctions can show relationships of time, reason, contrast, and purpose.

1. Time: when, whenever
2. Reason: because, since
3. Contrast: although, even though, though
4. Purpose: so that

Appendix 6

Transitions

Transitions are words or phrases that show the relationship between two ideas. The most common transitions are used to:

1. Give examples: for example, for instance
2. Add emphasis: in fact, of course
3. Add information: in addition, furthermore, moreover, besides
4. Make comparisons: similarly, likewise
5. Show contrast: however, nevertheless, in contrast, on the contrary, on one/on the other hand
6. Give reasons or results: therefore, as a result, as a consequence, for this/that reason
7. Show sequences: now, then, first (second, etc.) earlier, later, meanwhile, finally

Photo Credits for Writing:
Interactions 1 ©2007

Page 3: © Digital Vision/Getty Images; 4: © Royalty-Free/CORBIS; 9: © Digital Vision/ SuperStock; 16: © BananaStock/JupiterImages; 18: © Everett Collection; 21: © Digital Vision/PunchStock; 41: © Creatas/SuperStock; 42: © Tom Wilson/Getty Images;; 43: © Royalty-Free/CORBIS; 51: © Michael Lamotte/Cole Group/Getty Images; 52: © Nancy R. Cohen/Getty Images; 59: © D. Normark/PhotoLink/Getty Images; 61 (top left): © Ryan McVay/Getty Images; 60 (top right): © Neil Beer/Getty Images; 60 (middle left): © Getty Images/Digital Vision; 60 (middle right): © RubberBall Productions/Getty Images; 60 (bottom): © C. McIntyre/PhotoLink/Getty Images; 63: © McGraw-Hill Companies, Inc./Gary He, photographer; 64: © Comstock Images/ Jupiter Images; 74, 77, 80: © Royalty-Free/ CORBIS; 83: © Earl & Nazima Kowall/ CORBIS; 90: Library of Congress; 93: © Bob Rowan; Progressive Image/CORBIS; 109, 110 (top left): © Dynamic Graphics/JupiterImages; 110 (top right, bottom right): © Royalty-Free/CORBIS; 110 (bottom left): © Tracy Montana/ PhotoLink/Getty Images; 120, 125: © Walter Gilardetti; 127: © Najlah Feanny/CORBIS; 128 (all): © Everett Collection; 129 (top left): © Miramax/courtesy Everett Collection; 129 (top right): © Everett Collection; 129 (bottom): © CORBIS SYGMA; 136L © Joaquin Palting/ Getty Images; 142: © The McGraw-Hill Companies, Inc./Lars Niki, photographer; 145: © Ariel Skelley/CORBIS; 150: © PhotoDisc; 153, 154: © Dynamic Graphics/JupiterImages; 163: © Royalty-Free/CORBIS; 167 (both): © PhotoLink/Getty Images; 172: © Royalty-Free/CORBIS; 174: © PhotoLink/Getty Images; 175: © Ryan McVay/Getty Images; 178: © Royalty-Free/CORBIS.